Alaska Women Write

Alaska Women Write

Living, Laughing, and Loving on the Last Frontier

Edited by Dana Stabenow

Foreword by Libby Riddles

EPICENTER PRESS • *Alaska Book Adventures*

Epicenter Press is a regional press founded in Alaska whose interests include but are not limited to the arts, history, environment, and diverse cultures and lifestyles of the Pacific Northwest and high latitudes. We seek both the traditional and innovative in publishing nonfiction books, and contemporary art and photography gift books.

Publisher: Kent Sturgis
Editor: Dana Stabenow
Cover and Book Design: Victoria Sturgis
Map: Marge Mueller, Gray Mouse Graphics
Proofreader: Sherrill Carlson
Printer: Haagen Printing
Bindery: Lincoln & Allen Co.

Library of Congress Control Number: 2003105386

ISBN 0-9708493-8-9

Booksellers: This title is available from major wholesalers. Retail discounts are available from our trade distributor, Graphic Arts Center Publishing Co., PO Box 10306, Portland, OR 97210. Phone 800-452-3032.

PRINTED IN THE UNITED STATES OF AMERICA

First Edition
First Printing, May 2003

10 9 8 7 6 5 4 3 2 1

To order single copies of ALASKA WOMEN WRITE, mail $14.95 plus $4.95 for shipping (WA residents add $1.30 state sales tax) to: Epicenter Press, PO Box 82368, Kenmore, WA 98028.

Discover exciting ALASKA BOOK ADVENTURES! Visit our online Alaska bookstore at www.EpicenterPress.com, or call our 24-hour, toll-free hotline at 800-950-6663. Visit our online gallery for Iditarod artist Jon Van Zyle at www.JonVanZyle.com.

Either write something worth reading or do
something worth writing.

— *Benjamin Franklin*

Foreword

Most of you have read the stories of grand adventure in Alaska, heroic stories of the native peoples and early adventurers in this rough and legend-inspiring land. Alaska is a place like no other, and its harsh beauty shapes the people who make their home here.

Years ago when I moved here as a green kid from Minnesota, I would laugh at my parents when they told me I should write a book about my experience of living in Alaska. I thought it was absurd; sure, I'd been out homesteading in western Alaska, but compared to the people I met, my story at the time was just unfolding. It would be years and an Iditarod championship later when I finally felt I had something worth writing about.

The stories I had read about Alaska had given me invaluable insight about life in the north, but it was hard not to notice that almost all of the stories were written by or about men. The stories I heard of Alaskan women were more likely to be in conversation than in print. There were wonderful tales of women catching moose by themselves or living out in the Bush or teaching in villages. Women drawn to Alaska for reasons of their own or following their men, but shaped by Alaska and its intense weather and terrain. These were great stories to which I could easily relate.

Some of those stories you now hold in your hand. How to Pack for an Earthquake chronicles the funny, sad, inspirational and frustrating events that often cause an Alaskan woman to ask herself "Why is it I live here? Why am I doing this?" And often, "Will I survive?"

Alaska provides unique experiences for self-discovery in which women have learned to love, hate, and tolerate the Last Frontier, finally calling it home.

I hope you enjoy this collection as much as I have. ⤶

Libby Riddles

Libby Riddles is author of *Race Across Alaska — First Woman to Win the Iditarod Tells Her Story*, *Danger the Dog yard Cat*, and *Storm Run*.

Table of Contents

❧

*Soloing consists of three
consecutive takeoffs and,
worse, landings. I envisioned
Rick hovering over the air traffic
controller with all of his fingers
crossed. I would've crossed
my own, except that I needed
both hands to fly the plane.*

Linda Billington

My One-Night Stand with the Air

She could fly but she couldn't land

by Linda Billington

Linda Billington arrived in Alaska back in the Cretaceous Period, also known as 1969 or The Year Big Oil Leased the North Slope. She spent the next 26 years as a reporter and editor for the *Anchorage Daily News*, covering such diverse characters as Richard M. Nixon and Ronald McDonald and the crazy folks who leap into Resurrection Bay every January. Since retiring, she has devoted her time to travel, working (slooooooowly) on an Alaskan suspense novel, and taking a fortunately short-lived stab at piloting. ✒

I COULD FLY JUST FINE.

I just couldn't land.

That pretty much sums up my short, inglorious career as an Alaskan student pilot.

Rick, my instructor, was the soul of patience and encouragement. With his lanky frame folded into the right-hand seat of the Cessna 152, he'd gently guide me through the complexities of aviation.

Then one day he directed me to land on the shorter of two runways at Merrill Field. Merrill is a busy general-aviation airport smack on the fringe of downtown Anchorage, Alaska. All kinds of aircraft weighing 12,500 pounds or less come in there, and they come in from several directions. My preference — because it was both long and wide — was runway 6/24. Runway 15/33 was one thousand three hundred and fifty feet shorter. And the approach to 15/33 came in so low over car traffic that I just knew I'd take the top off that red SUV cruising down Fifteenth Avenue.

As usual, Rick talked me down calmly: "Okay, level those wings. Good. Remember, keep it straight with the rudder, not the control wheel. You're a little high; ease off on the throttle a bit. Okay, now back to idle. Right ... Now, level off."

We swooped across the end of the runway and the plane started to sink and I was trying to recall just when I should bring the nose up and suddenly Rick's calm instructions were growing staccato: "Nose up, now — nose up — nose UP more more MORE!" And we hit, and bounced, and bounced again, and I figured hey, we're down, and dropped the nose wheel just as we bounced a third time.

"Fuck!" Rich said, the first and only explicit Anglo-Saxonism I'd ever heard from his mouth. Later he told me that I could have demolished the nose wheel. But once we'd braked and moved onto the taxiway and I'd caught my breath, all he said was, "Well, we'd better get the mechanic to check out the landing gear."

We did, and the mechanic did, and we went up again. And the next time we came down okay. But I knew then that landing was never going to be my forte.

Oh, I tried. I bought books on good landings. I watched videotapes of good landings. I tried to get into the landing zone, if there is such a place. No luck.

A landing at Merrill was one of the first things I saw my first day in Anchorage. Fueled by an overdose of Jack London and Robert Service and Rex Beach, in nineteen sixty-nine I took a reporting job at the Anchorage Daily News, loaded my earthly possessions and a friend into a four-year-old Plymouth Barracuda, and headed up the Alcan. Eleven days later, we entered Anchorage.

Cruising into town, I was startled by a tiny single-engine plane that roared over my car low enough to sear the gold paint off the chassis. Then I realized that the plane was aiming for an airfield that paralleled the highway just a few feet away.

I had discovered Merrill Field.

For nearly forty years, Merrill had served as a major link to the Alaska beyond the skimpy road system. The airplane, I quickly discovered, was the pickup truck of these northern skies, the battered everyday workhorse decked in worn paint, its dings patched with ingenuity and duct tape. Never before had I lived in a place where small planes were taken so much for granted, where flight was not just a reality, but a daily necessity.

I just had to try this flying business.

Signing up with a local flight school, I managed a couple of lessons in a little Cessna 150. Swiftly I was slapped in the face by three sobering facts:

(a) I couldn't afford it,

(b) I was acrophobic, and

(c) I was scared to death that I could die up there — or, worse, kill someone else.

(c) was the chief problem. I didn't touch an airplane's controls again for nearly thirty years.

I flew, but only as a passenger. Lay a map of Alaska over the South 48 and Alaska will extend over both borders and both coasts. The air lanes are the only routes to many remote sites. And as an occasionally roving reporter, I had a built-in excuse to indulge my passion for planes. Cessnas and Grummans ferried me to the brown bears at McNeil River and over the ice fields of Kachemak Bay. Jets carried me to coastal towns like Nome, Kotzebue, Bethel and Barrow, and to the glorious green hills of Kodiak. Float planes put me down on water like glass and waves choppy enough to make Ahab toss his cookies. A helicopter once took me on a Bush journey to find an abandoned horse.

Despite that empty air between me and the earth, I loved it all, even when my fingers bent the armrests, even when I gasped at each bump in the clouds, even when the private pilot who flew me to Valdez neglected to warn me that his landing technique involved stalling out well above the runway, dropping straight down, and hitting hard — the hell with the undercarriage.

So, shortly past my fifty-fourth birthday, I returned to Merrill Field to try again. By then, Anchorage had grown, and so had the little downtown airport. Alaska was home to nearly 10,000 general aviation aircraft, nine hundred of which were based at Merrill. Just the previous year, the field had been ranked the 96th busiest airport in the United States, with 187,190 flight operations.

Once again I signed up with a flight school. This time the rental planes were Cessna 152s. Rick-the-instructor was half my age, half again my height, and very much into the zen of flying. In the plane's left seat, with Rick beside me, I was almost fine most of the time. Takeoffs were a cinch. I'd point the Cessna down the runway's center line, give it full throttle, and when it reached the right speed, raise the nose. The plane just flew itself off the ground. Granted, I always had trouble with the center line part. Despite Rick's repeated chants of "More right rudder," I tended to drift to the left. This, I understood, had to do with something called torque. But hey, I figured if the wheels were on the pavement rather than on the grass, we were okay.

Once in the air, I had little trouble maintaining altitude, controlling airspeed, maneuvering and turning. Rick said I flew to commercial standards. He was an encouraging soul.

Generally we flew west, across the Turnagain Arm of Cook Inlet to the farmlands spread out like drying blankets in the shadow of Mount Susitna. It's a good place to practice, with all those acres of flat available in case of an emergency landing. I didn't like thinking of emergency landings, but appreciated the precautions. I also appreciated the irony when I learned that the best place for an emergency touch-down in town near Merrill Field was the municipal cemetery.

Of course, we weren't alone in the sky. Not only is Merrill one of the busiest airports in the country, but it's flanked to the south by Anchorage International Airport and to the north by Elmendorf Air Force Base. Traffic roars in from all directions, at all altitudes, all the time. I had to keep an eye out for bulky 747s, wasplike F15s, lumbering C-5A cargo haulers, and everything else that could produce a dangerous wake. When you're riding a tiny C-152, Mister Turbulence is not your friend. The whole idea of flying is to keep the blue side UP.

It took a while before I could start picking my Cessna's ID from the controller and pilot chatter rattling in over the headset: "Seven Six Seven, be advised of a heavy westbound at five thousand ... Three Tango Yankee, you're at fifteen hundred; you going to stay there for a while? ... Seven Golf Quebec, watch for the Beechcraft at one o'clock."

Who? Seven Golf what? Damn, that's me!

"Seven Golf Quebec, looking for traffic." Where's the Beech? Is that it? Nope, that's a speck on the windscreen. Where IS that plane? Do those controllers know what they're talking about? If I can't find it, are we going to do a head-on? Here, Beech; here, baby, come to mama. Damn! It's gotta be somewhere ... Oh, there it is.

Of course, eventually I always had to go home to Merrill. But the trouble with landing is that it's nothing like taking off. Takeoff is no more complicated, really, than negotiating the Seward Highway at rush hour. Landing requires focusing on a lot more details, many of them simultaneously. I just couldn't get them all right at the same time. If my final turn was made at the correct speed, my altitude was off or I wasn't lined up with the runway or I couldn't keep up with the tower's instructions or I had to double-check my flaps or I couldn't recall if I'd turned on the carburetor heat. On top of all that, I had to throttle back to idle at a certain point, level off at a certain point, bring the nose up at a certain point — and, with luck and skill, settle to the ground like a wisp of down from a Canada goose.

Hah.

Meanwhile, I was building up my hours. Average time to the first solo flight is about fifteen hours. I passed that mark. Figured I could solo in twenty. No such luck. Aimed for twenty-five. By thirty I still didn't feel ready — not so much because I couldn't handle the plane in the air as because I was afraid to come down.

In the interim, I discovered that my goal had changed. I'd started off aiming for a private pilot's license, but I hadn't envisioned much beyond that. As the lessons continued, so did the drain on my bank account, and I began to realize that flying was going to be one expensive hobby. Even if I got my license, I'd still have to fly a minimum number of hours every year to please the FAA. It was unlikely that I'd ever be able to afford my own plane, or even a piece of one, or hourly rental fees.

Finally, the truth clouted me upside the head. Yes, I'd always wanted to pilot a plane, but I didn't have to marry the air. I didn't need a lifelong commitment; a one-night stand would do. I just wanted to solo, to be up there one time with the plane and my own abilities and my own shaky nerves, and see if I could get through it without killing myself or anyone else.

Winter was looming and I really wanted to solo before snow covered the ground. I had more than enough trouble landing on dry pavement. A couple of snowfalls came and melted away, and by early November I knew winterlong ground cover was imminent.

November 11, under a dark gray ceiling, Rick and I took a few passes around the field. The overcast was high enough to show Mount McKinley all alpenglowed in the afternoon. Astonishingly, to her left was a wondrous sight: a Fata Morgana, an illusory range of rocky buttresses created from light. We gasped and wondered. It looked like an omen, a marvelously magical one.

I went around a few times, touching and going, and tackled the dreaded runway 15/33. That time I made one of my best landings ever.

"You're ready," Rick said.

I dithered, but finally agreed: "Let's do it."

"Drop me off at the control tower," he said.

Soloing consists of three consecutive takeoffs and, worse, landings. Fortunately, I was on the longer runway, in Seven Golf Quebec, my favorite plane, and Merrill tower was aware that a nervous novice was at the controls. I envisioned Rick hovering over the air traffic controller with all of his fingers crossed. I would've crossed my own, except that I needed both hands to fly the plane.

"Seven Golf Quebec clear for takeoff," said the controller, and the Cessna and I roared down the runway, cheerfully left of center. I brought up the nose and we took flight together.

From then on, I was too busy to worry, too busy focusing on reaching five hundred feet before turning crosswind, too busy trying to level off at nine hundred while turning down-wind parallel to the runway, too busy remembering to put on the carb heat and throttle back to seventeen hundred as I passed the far end of the runway, too busy putting in ten degrees of flaps when the needle hit eighty, too busy marking the point where I'd make my base turn (the landmark for that, coincidentally, being my old workplace, the Anchorage Daily News), too busy watching my altitude and airspeed and putting in more flaps at certain points and turning into the final approach and lining up with the runway and making sure I wasn't too high or too low and keeping my wings level and steering with the rudder and throttling back to idle at the right time and leveling off at the right time and bringing the nose up at the right time. . .

And making my worst landing since the day I'd caused Rick to curse.

But this time at least I knew what to do and didn't abuse the nose wheel, although I'd been so focused on everything else that I'd forgotten the damned right rudder again and Seven Golf Quebec and I were cruising down the runway well to the left of the center line and heading almost to-ward the base of the tower before I got her straightened out again, raised the flaps, cut the carb heat and throttled full power for the second takeoff.

The next two landings were a lot better. They weren't pret-tier, but they were softer, and I didn't head for the tower again, either. But I was so relieved after the final one that when the controller told me to take the left-hand taxiway, I followed habit and took the right one instead, winding up on the opposite side of the runway from where Rick waited to be picked up.

When I finally taxied across the field to him, he looked a bit shaky, but relieved. "Congratulations," he said. Then, softly: "Got a little close to the tower on that first landing."

As I tied down Seven Golf Quebec back at the flight service lot, I glanced up at the clouds. A snowflake drifted down and hit me on the nose.

My career as a pilot was over. Once more the skies were safe for general aviation.

But, by God, I'd flown. ⤚

❧

Despite my weary muscles,
my step is light as I stroll home
across the frozen lagoon. I think
I must be the first white woman
to ever sew a seam on a umiaq.

Karen Brewster

Amiqing

Sewing a sealskin whaleboat

by Karen Brewster

Karen Brewster moved to Alaska in 1988 from the San Francisco Bay Area. She lived in Barrow from 1989 to 1997, where she worked on a subsistence harvest study and was the Oral Historian for the North Slope Borough's Inupiat History, Language and Culture Commission. This provided a wonderful opportunity for her to get to know Inupiaq elders and to learn about their lives, their history, and their culture. Karen also participated in Barrow's cultural activities, such as being on a whaling crew and learning to sew skins. Karen completed a Masters Degree in Oral History at the University of Alaska-Fairbanks (UAF) in 1998. Currently, she is a Research Associate with the Oral History Program at UAF's Elmer E. Rasmuson Library. Previous publications include *Alaska Geographic*, Arctic, and North Slope Borough educational/cultural brochures. ᥒ

I CAN'T HELP BUT NOTICE the smell as I step into the qanitchaq, the enclosed porch that keeps cold air from entering the house. The full effect of the potent odor, reminiscent of rotten meat, smacks me in the face as I open the front door. My eyes water. I choke on my first breath, as I try to say hello to the fifteen people crowded into Eugene and Charlotte's narrow, rectangular living room.

It is March in Barrow. Time to sew bearded seal skins together to cover the umiaq, the skin boat the North Alaskan Inupiaq Eskimo use for whaling. "You know it's spring time when you smell it," a whaler told me once, referring to the strong scent of these skins. The bowhead whales do not arrive until late April or early May, but in preparation whaling crew members clean old meat and blubber out of underground ice cellars, repair harpoons, guns, paddles, sleds, and snowmachines, and replace boat covers so the hides will have plenty of time to dry and bleach white in the bright sun of the lengthening days.

This is not my first experience with the sights, sounds and smells of amiqing, the Inupiaq word for boat-cover sewing. I moved to Barrow in June 1989 from Anchorage, when I was twenty-five, to conclude a federally funded project documenting the community's hunting and fishing activities. Before the year was over, I decided I liked Barrow and wanted to stay. When the project ended, I found a new job as the Oral Historian for the North Slope Borough Commission on Inupiat History, Language and Culture. I hoped to help document old ways of doing things that fewer and fewer people still knew how to do. One way I learned about Inupiaq culture was to immerse myself, to watch and to listen. Every spring I went to one of the whaling captain's houses to observe a boat-sewing session.

The women's powerful hands pushed sharp needles into one-and-a-half-inch thick skins and pulled long threads through their stitches. As a non-Native newcomer to Barrow, I did not want to be intrusive, so I sat on the sidelines. I shyly and quietly asked for explanations. The longer I sat surrounded by the odor of the slick and oily ugruk skins, the less I noticed it. Despite five years of this, the smell was overpowering every spring when I met it again.

Today, the two blue leather overstuffed couches in Eugene and Charlotte's living room are pushed up against the outer walls. They are covered with old bed sheets and plastic sheeting. The dining room table and six blue/gray upholstered, padded arm chairs on wheels are crowded into the kitchen, leaving little room to maneuver around them to get to the refrigerator, stove, sink, or the coffee pot on the far counter. Sheets of clear plastic Visqueen are taped over the floor to protect the beige linoleum from the seal oil that oozes from the limp and slimy skins piled in the center of the room. The floor is also covered with cardboard — boxes cut open to lie flat — to keep us from slipping.

Cora, Bertha, Hester, Margaret, Dorothy, Isabelle, Mary, Eunice, Emma, Flora and Rebecca sit around the kitchen table drinking coffee and smoking cigarettes. They speak rapidly in Inupiaq. Despite years of trying to learn this complicated language, I only catch a familiar word here and there. I guess they are sharing funny stories when raucous laughter runs around the circle.

As they visit, the women prepare their sewing equipment. In between cigarette puffs, Hester, now in her seventies, skinny and coughing from a lifetime of smoking, cuts head and arm holes into a large, black Hefty trash bag. Eighty-year-old Bertha, the oldest of the group, pulls her plastic poncho over her head, wide shoulders, and short and stout body to cover her clothes. Isabelle, in her late forties with fly-away permed black hair, circular glasses, and a contagious laugh, sits on a chair and carefully draws white trash bags over her slim legs.

"What a good ad for Hefty bags," Flora jokes. Everyone giggles.

Cora, herself a whaling captain since her husband died, is in her late seventies and doesn't say much other than to give directions in Inupiaq. She snips the feet off old, dingy-white sweat socks and pulls the socks up her arms as sleeves. Her daughter Margaret, who towers 5'9" tall, is dark-skinned and still strikingly beautiful at fifty. She cuts navy blue bias tape into strips to tie up their leggings and sleeves. All this serves as a barrier against the ever-pervading seal oil and smell.

Once you've been in the room with these skins, you smell like rotten ugruk whether you've touched them or not. The smell hangs thick in the air, permeating every fabric, every pore, every hair like cigarette smoke at a bar. It lingers on you for hours.

Once they're each fully outfitted, the women gather up needles, metal thimbles, and finger-guards. Dorothy secures her homemade leather finger-cover to her right hand to protect herself from needle pokes and the coarse thread rubbing against her skin. She appears to be in her late sixties, with a blue bandana tied over her gray permed hair, and trim, drawn-on brown eyebrows arching above her thick, purple-framed glasses. Bertha searches her sewing kit for her favorite thimble. Flora, who is 5'4" tall, stocky and athletic, tries on various thimbles and finger protectors borrowed from others until she finds ones that fit her thick hands. As a young beginner — only thirty-five — she does not yet have her own set-up. The women are now ready to begin.

There are seven ugruk skins to sew together, which means six seams. Pairs of women sit across the skins from each other, one at each seam. Each starts at the middle and sews to the outer edge. Today, they need twelve women. They are short-handed.

"Karen, what about you?" Bertha asks in her heavy Inupiaq accent.

"Well, I don't know." I am flattered by the offer and her confidence. "I just stopped by to watch."

Sewing a boat is a big responsibility. After years of observing, I tried stitching on scraps the year before, but had not done it for real. Unlike the Inupiat who learn something by watching and then doing it, I need to repeatedly try before leaping into a new task. I'd joked about making a bathtub toy-sized umiaq to test the seaworthiness of my stitches, but I'd never found the time. Now, men's lives are on the line if my stitches don't hold.

Although I'd been sewing skins for a few years, I didn't have the best track record. During my first winter in Barrow, I took a community education class in skin sewing. My first project was a pair of sheepskin overmitts to keep my hands warm when snowmachining. My ignorance of basic sewing was obvious when I ended up with two right-handed mittens. Jane, the Inupiaq elder instructor, laughed as she explained, "You have to flip the pattern over for the left hand!"

Undeterred, I repeated the class two more times. I enjoyed the creative process of sewing skins into useful pieces of clothing. As my skills improved and with lots of help from Bertha, the new instructor, I made a furry beaver hat that looks like a gorilla's head when I wear it, seal-skin slippers, calf-skin baby booties, and a pair of knee-high sealskin mukluks with stiff and tough dried ugruk soles. As I did more sewing I grew increasingly interested in sewing techniques and how umiaq covers were made.

"You've been watching. You know what to do," Bertha says.

"Well, if you'll show me. And if it's OK with Eugene." Eugene is the captain of the Aalaak whaling crew, for whom this boat cover is being made. Each whaling crew is named. Eugene utilizes his Inupiaq name, Aalaak. As a member of his crew for the previous four years, I want to be sure I show proper respect and ask permission. It means letting a beginner, an outsider, work on his boat. He and his crew will be at the mercy of my stitches.

"Sure, go ahead," Eugene says with a grin, as he oversees and directs the day's activities.

This is Flora's first time umiaq sewing, as well. I feel less pressure not being the only novice.

"OK, I'll try it," I say.

I don't really feel I can say no. It is an honor to be asked by such respected sewers. Not all the women in Barrow know how to sew the umiaq's special waterproof stitch. There is a select group of twelve to fifteen women who work on all of Barrow's skin boats. There are over forty registered whaling crews in Barrow, but they do not all cover their boats every year. In order to participate in a whaling season, a whaling crew must sign up with the Alaska Eskimo Whaling Commission, the local organization that oversees the hunt and ensures the number of whales taken does not exceed the quota allotted by the International Whaling Commission. Typically, a skin cover lasts two to three seasons, if well cared for or not converted into the trampoline-like blanket used at Nalukataq, the end of the whaling season celebration. Ten to twenty boats usually need to be covered each spring. Day after day, the sewing groups hop from crew to crew, from boat to boat. They have barely enough time in between gigs to relax sore muscles, sleep, and wash clothes. Sometimes they work on as many as seven boats in seven days.

Living in Barrow, I came to understand that the continued use of handmade wood-framed skin boats for spring whaling still serves a purpose. I learned that these lightweight boats could easily be pulled on a sled behind a snowmachine out to the ice edge or pushed into the water by a handful of men. They moved smoothly and quietly in the water, and so were less likely than the noisy aluminum boats to scare the whales. Their skin covering was tough and durable.

I became intrigued by these boats and wanted to know how they were made. During mid-winter evenings in Barrow, I sometimes stopped at the woodshop and watched the men put the umiaq frames together. They built the keel with cut lumber. They shaped the bow piece from a driftwood tree stump. I don't know why the folks of Barrow put up with me. "You always ask too many questions," they'd tease. But, they let me stay and watch.

Now that I've agreed to try boat sewing, I rush into the kitchen and quickly make my own plastic dress, leggings, and sock sleeves. I remove my watch, but think nothing of the gray, frayed, braided rope bracelet that's wound around my right wrist since childhood. My sister and I have kept these bracelets on no matter what, despite our mother's disgust at their grubby and "unladylike" appearance. I frantically search through sewing kits for a metal thimble small enough for my kid-sized finger. I finally find one in Bertha's sewing pouch. I hurriedly cut the fingertips off an old leather baseball batting glove, and put it on my right hand to protect my fingers. I don't want to keep the ladies waiting.

As I prepare myself, Charlie, George and Eugene work on the pale pinkish-gray skins lying on the floor. Charlie is one of

Eugene's younger brothers – Eugene is fifty, Charlie in his late forties – and George is married to their cousin. All three have been whaling since they were boys, and on the same crew since Eugene's father put it together in the 1970s.

Eugene drags the biggest skin to the middle of the floor. "George, put that one over there," he says, pointing to a thin skin with a small hole in it. It will be at the boat's bow end, where it receives less wear and tear. George peers out from under his baseball cap with a blank, sleepy stare, not quite awake at 9:30 on a Saturday morning. Eugene's command jolts him awake and he jumps into action.

After a long discussion in Inupiaq, Charlie and George pick up each skin and pull hard on the ends until the skin is taut. They lean back away from each other to get the most tension, grimacing from the strain. Charlie's paunch protrudes over the top of his baggy royal-blue sweats with Barrow Whalers—the high school basketball team—emblazoned down the left leg in bright yellow lettering. Eugene grabs a sharp knife in his right hand and cuts across the skin from flipper to flipper to create a straight edge for sewing. "Pull harder," Eugene snaps as the skin begins to sag. His round face and big eyes focus intently on his work. The older women call out commands in Inupiaq to make sure the guys place and cut the skins correctly.

Now it is time to take our positions. The women have already chosen their partners and figured out who gets which seam. They put the beginners near the ends, less critical spots on the boat, and give us experienced partners. I am directed to sit at the second seam back from the bow, across from my teacher, Bertha, and in between Emma and Mary. Emma, although only in her forties, has been sewing for enough years to be well skilled in the art. She has straight, long black hair, pulled back into a ponytail today. Her large eyes brighten her face when she laughs, which she does often. Mary, in her late seventies and an expert sewer of parkas, boots, hats, and boat covers, quietly and proudly sits on my other side to keep an eye on me in case I run into trouble.

The others are already sitting on the floor, lined up along each edge of the skins. Slowly, one woman, then another lifts up the heavy blanket of moist, slippery hide and heavyweight clear plastic underneath it and stretches her legs straight out in front of her. The skins lie across our laps like the lead X-ray vests used in dentist offices.

A lot of preparation goes into getting everything ready for amiqing. Each July and August, women butcher seals and wrap the hides, hair side in, around pieces of blubber for storage. After eight months of self-rendering, the hair easily falls off when men scrape the skins smooth a few days prior to sewing. Women spend all winter making thread. They strip and soak caribou legs, rip out the tendons, peel and dry the sinew, and braid the sinew strands together into some of the toughest thread you'll ever find. One piece of braided thread, measured two times across the chest from fingertip to fingertip, is used for each seam.

Bertha secures the thread's mid-point at a spot on the skin halfway between us. She tosses one end of the thread to me and keeps the other for herself. Each end is thinned to a single strand slender enough to run through the tiny eye of a needle. I take my size nine, three-sided skin sewing needle from the front of my plastic outerwear, where I skewered it for safekeeping, and begin the challenging task of threading it. "Be careful with the end," Bertha scolds. Her deep voice echoes through the silence of the focused group.

"If it soaks up too much oil it's more likely to break and will be harder to thread the next time." Emma explains in a soothing voice. "Try not to handle the thread end too much or let it lie on the skin."

While I am still squinting and trying to line up the needle's eye with the thread, Cora, Dorothy, Mary, Bertha, and Eunice have already started sewing on the middle seams. I am behind and I haven't even started yet.

I am handicapped from the outset by my slow sewing speed. Some of these women have been sewing for seventy years. The fact that we don't start stitching at the same time puts me at an even greater disadvantage. I worry about being the last to finish. I don't want to give them a reason to regret inviting me into their circle.

I watch Bertha. Her stout fingers plunge the needle into the thick hide in a straight running stitch parallel to the seam. She is careful to go only through the top layer of skin so she won't lose the waterproof quality of the stitches. Bertha pulls and pulls the long thread with her right hand until the stitch is snug. She starts the next stitch directly across the seam from where the needle came out. She pushes the needle down with the metal thimble on her right forefinger. The flowery pattern stamped into the outside of the thimble is worn smooth from use. Bertha then takes the needle back across the seam to the first skin to start the cycle again. This double-stitch creates an overlapping flap that is sewn down on the skins' backside. This forms a channel that acts as a waterproof barrier. Bertha's wide hands work quickly as she proceeds down the seam from the tips of her toes towards her knees. From her swift movements you'd never guess she is eighty years old.

I try a stitch of my own. The skin is dense and tough. It feels like wet human flesh. I have trouble pushing the needle through. Bertha makes it look easy. I push as hard as I can with my thimbled first finger, then pull, pull, pull the long thread through, trying to get that just right tension on the stitch that I've been told is so important.

I glance at Mary, the elder expert, on my right to see how she is sewing. Then I watch Emma at my left. I want to make sure I am doing it right. I ask out loud, not directed to anyone in particular, "How tight should I pull the thread?"

"Until it's just right," Mary replies. "Your stitches should be bigger," she corrects as I poke my needle farther along into the skin. "But, not too big," she scolds. I pull the needle back out to make a shorter span. Mary nods in affirmation. The corners of her small mouth rise into a smile.

I struggle to keep a grip on the slippery skins, to hold the seam closed with my left hand. I tighten the stitch by yanking on the thread in short spurts. I fight to keep the four-foot-long thread from getting tangled and knotted. Don't push the needle all the way through the skin. Keep the stitches even. Line the stitches up directly across the seam from each other. I squirm. I sigh. I groan in frustration.

"Are you doing OK down there, Karen?" Isabelle asks calmly. Her concern comforts me.

"Yeah," I reply quietly, not wanting to show weakness. "This sure is hard work, though." The other women smile.

"You know, it would be easier if you straightened your legs out in front of you and used your feet to hold up the part of the seam you're working on. Like this," Mary suggests as she wiggles her small upturned feet back and forth under the skin. Mary is 5'4" and though in her late seventies her tight-curled permed, short hair is only a mottled gray, the black color of youth still obvious.

"I can't reach the end of my toes if I stretch my legs out." I lean forward to show them. "I'm too tall."

At 5'7", I am two to five inches taller than most of the Inupiaq women sewing around me. I demonstrate how I have to bend my knees out to the sides to reach the beginning of my seam in the skins hanging over my feet. I wonder how Margaret, who is taller than me, can do it. Giggles spread through the group like the latest hot gossip.

It's an Inupiaq quilting bee, interrupted only by periodic gossip, jokes, and stories. "Remember that spring we went camping and I fell off the back of the sled?" Eunice says. She has been concentrating hard on sewing and has not said much all day. "We were up inland geese hunting. My husband was driving the ski-doo. We were on our honeymoon. He drove off quickly and I wasn't holding on good enough. I went flying off that sled! There I was sitting on the ground. Wondering where the sled had gone to." Eunice giggles over the fifty-year-old memory.

High-pitched, off-key Inupiaq gospel singing flows from the stereo. Cora hums along in a gravely alto. Emma chimes in on a chorus now and again with a high-pitched and lively soprano. Eugene's three daughters, in their late teens and early twenties, hang around the edges of the room. They bring us tea, coffee, soda, or water, and they pass paper towels and ulu knives when we ask. Their younger eyes and dry fingers come in handy for needle re-threading. I try not to ask for much. I am only thirty years old and feel awkward being waited on. Usually, I am one of the young ones helping the elders.

After four hours of sewing, of sitting on the floor with my legs in front of me and not leaning against anything, I finish the first side of my seam. I am exhausted. I think Mary glanced out the side of her glasses periodically to check that I was doing things right. At least, I hope she did.

All the experienced women have finished before me and are eating the lunch that Eugene provided. They eat hot caribou soup, bread, dried fish, chunks of frozen whale blubber known as maktak, and other Inupiaq delicacies.

I wiggle out from under the lap blanket of skins and realize they are done with their break and anxious to start sewing again. They've been waiting for us slow pokes. All of the front seams have to be finished before anyone can start on the back side. The men flip the skin covering as a single unit. Afraid of criticism and of holding everyone else up, I quickly slurp a bowl of soup and chomp a piece of homemade white bread. It's just like being the slowest hiker on a backpacking trip. By the time you catch up with everyone else, they've had a long rest while waiting and are ready to start walking again. You barely have a chance to catch your breath and gulp a swig of water before they're off. The lack of rest only makes you slower than before.

I return to the floor and to sewing without time to relieve my sore back or uncramp my fingers. Each woman sews the front and back of the same seam, so with the skins flipped my seam is now on the opposite side of the room. I sit where Bertha was all morning, and she's in my old spot. Again, Bertha marks the middle, measures the thread, and secures it with a special sewn-on knot. On this side, the thread and seam are constantly swathed with chunks of thawed seal blubber, called uqsruq in Inupiaq. The seal oil permeates the thread, the moisture expands the sinew, and it fills up the needle hole tighter. This keeps the stitch watertight.

"Uqsruq!" Margaret exclaims, directing that the bowl of fat be passed to her. Margaret is one of the few women in town who goes out whaling. She camps on the ice for a month or more, hunts, and works alongside her brothers to run their family's crew.

Like a chant and its echo, a few minutes later Bertha asks, "Pass the uqsruq." Back and forth calls continue throughout the afternoon.

The blubber rubbing makes this side more slippery than the first. The slimy pile is too much for my small, inexperienced hands. I keep losing my grip. I flop over the three-inch flap of skin that is left from the overlap on the front. I try to sew it down over the back seam with a regular skin sewing stitch: through the top skin and across the seam to the other skin all in one needle thrust. I concentrate on my work. The leather glove has worn through at the crook of my forefinger. Each pull of the thread hurts more and more, as the coarse sinew runs across my exposed and cracked skin.

For some reason, sewing on the backside trips me up. I have done enough other skin sewing that I know the stitch, but I can't get the angle right. I can't brace the seam against my feet. The skins slip from my grasp, and the seam spreads open. Like cheating on a final exam, I peer over to find answers in Emma's work. It looks like she is doing something different, but I can't figure out what. Why am I so awkward? What am I doing wrong?

Mary notices my anxiousness. "Just do your own. You're doing fine," she says reassuringly. I appreciate her confidence but still feel clumsy.

About halfway down the seam I find my groove. After seven hours of sewing, I finally feel like I've got the hang of it. I am proud that I persevered. Then I round the curve of my seam at the outer edge and the thin thread breaks and my needle comes off. After five minutes, and a lot of swearing under my breath, I finally get it re-threaded. I make a few more stitches and the needle comes off again. "Shit," I cry angrily.

I have pulled on the needle too much instead of on the thread, and the tension has caused the weakened oil-soaked end to break off. The thread tip is frayed and splitting, so each time it is harder to get the needle back on. My hands are so tired from gripping the heavy skins and holding the needle too tightly, that my sewing becomes painfully slow. I get farther and farther behind the rest of the group.

Many of the older, fast-sewing women are done already. They've peeled off their protective plastic layers and are sprawled on the couches drinking soda, smoking cigarettes, and resting their weary bones. It is five o'clock. Mary finishes her seam in tune with her peers. She hears my groans of frustration. She sees me struggling. She helps me re-thread for the fifth time.

"Go ahead. I'll finish it," Mary says in a soft, kind tone.

I am grateful and relieved. I am so tired that I've lost coordination in my hands. Each motion requires twice as much effort as before. I am on the verge of tears.

I extricate my legs from under the skins. I stand up slowly, like an old lady. My butt is numb and my back aches. How do these old women do it, I wonder. And, day after day sometimes. I guess your body must get used to it.

I hobble across the room still half hunched over. I remove my thimble, leather gloves, plastic bags, and arm socks. I wash my hands with mechanic's waterless cleaner to get rid of the grease and the smell, and put on my insulated overpants, fur-ruffed parka, heavy snow boots, hat and mittens for my walk home. I feel guilty for letting Mary finish my job. I am younger; I should stay and work harder. I should've kept trying, I think to myself. I feel like I've cheated.

When I try Inupiaq things, in the back of my mind I always figure because I am white I can get away with tiredness as a way out and not be chastised for being lazy. The elders don't expect as much from me as they do from Inupiaq women my age. They know I'm not as hardy, that I wasn't raised doing these things. But when it happens I feel like I'm taking advantage of this. The young Inupiaq women stay and finish, whether it is sewing skins, plucking geese, or cutting meat, no matter how long it takes or how tired they are.

But, after sitting all day hunched over those skins, the pain in my back and legs tells me I'm justified. And I know Mary will do a better job on the seam anyway.

"Thanks again for helping me, Mary," I say, hoping the extra appreciation will alleviate my guilt. I thank the rest of the ladies for allowing me to join them, and Eugene for the opportunity.

"Thanks for your help," Eugene calls to me from across the room as I grab the doorknob to leave.

"You did a good job," Bertha tells me, smiling proudly.

"I couldn't have done it without you," I say.

Despite my weary muscles, my step is light as I stroll home across the frozen lagoon. I think I must be the first white woman to ever sew a seam on an umiaq. I have no idea if this is true. After a day of being the only non-Inupiaq in the room, it sure feels that way. I am ecstatic that the women trust and like me enough to include me.

My newfound interest in sewing and the women's side of the Inupiaq hunting and fishing lifestyle surprises me. I grew up a tomboy with no desire to sew or do other things expected of girls and women of my suburban, middle-class culture. I preferred climbing trees, skateboarding, or making mud pies. The only sewing I did was in seventh grade home economics class where I made a terry cloth potholder, a red floral-print wrap-around skirt, and a white cotton lace blouse that never fit right. When I moved to Barrow, I was enthralled with Inupiaq culture and the people's ability to survive the severe Arctic climate. This usually translated into talk of men's hunting, men's knowledge of the landscape and the environment, men's flexibility to create or modify tools for specific uses, and the high-stakes world of whale hunting. Only after a few years did I start to notice and wonder what the women were doing.

I'd come to know that women not only create the umiaq covers but also sew warm parkas and boots, prepare food for the crew, provide logistics support at home base, cut up and distribute shares from the harvest, and organize and supervise all of the feasts.

"She's the boss," one captain explained to me about his wife's role. "I'm in charge out there on the ice. But once we hit land it's her."

When I got home, I took a shower, I washed my hair, and I laundered my clothes. But the foul odor of old ugruk stayed with me. Immersed in the smell all day, I'd become desensitized to it. But at home, like the contrast between cultures, the smell was obvious. I just couldn't figure out where it was coming from.

It wasn't until later that evening when I scratched an itch on my face that I realized the smell was coming from my rope bracelet. The sock sleeve had been insufficient protection; the bracelet had soaked up ugruk oil through the thin fabric for eight hours.

I tried everything to get the smell out. I smeared the rope with mechanic's Handgoop and rinsed it under hot water — twice. I even squeezed fresh lemon juice over my wrist, thinking that it works on fish smell. I was close to slicing the bracelet off when I remembered being told how a shot of Pinesol added to the laundry cut the grease and removed the ugruk smell. In my tired stupor, I grabbed the gallon jug of Pinesol and slowly poured some over my wrist. The fumes made my eyes water. I had to sleep with my arm stretched out away from me.

The ugruk perfume dissipated after a few days, but what I had accomplished that day soaked in to stay. I had proven my worth. I was not like other non-Natives who came and went, never showing interest or lingering long enough to learn. Eugene's crew caught a whale that year and used the boat cover for the Nalukataq blanket.

The following spring Eugene covered his boat again, and I was invited to help sew. This time I wrapped my wrist in plastic. ⮞

&

The pilot dropped us off
at Twin Lakes. That raw,
empty look that thrills me still,
everything windblown, barren,
fighting to stay alive in the
elements. Emptiness and
space. It was just us, and
the pilot was leaving.

Barbara Brown

Honeymoon

Not for her the honeymoon suite at the Plaza

by Barbara Brown

Barbara Brown, weekly columnist for the *Anchorage Daily News*, is better known to the 3- to 5-year-old set as "The Storytime Lady" from the Alaska Botanical Garden. To bigger kids, she's known as The Pronouncer for the Alaska State Spelling Bee—the person with those horrible words. She's been doing both those things since 1994. Barbara's first children's story, "Hanukkah in Alaska," was published in 1998 in the book *A Hanukkah Treasury*. She now works part-time for the Municipality of Anchorage, writing public information for the Library and Museum, and she is on the board of both the Anchorage Literacy Project and the Alaska Center for the Book.

MOST PEOPLE DECIDE to get married, choose a date, have a wedding, and then go on their honeymoon. Not us. Tim and I decided to go on a honeymoon, so we had to get married first. We skipped the wedding part entirely.

It was 1989, and I was working for Federal Express. Everyone else brought their spouses along on business trips because they had company flight benefits. Unfortunately, Tim was "only" my boyfriend, so he didn't count, no matter how long we'd been together. Things like this drive you crazy. Crazy enough to get married in order to get flight benefits.

No, that wasn't the only reason. But being a feminist-flower-child sort of woman, I was not a major fan of legalizing the marriage contract, although I was in love with a man who was. I think the flight benefits bit was a middle ground, a first compromise on the way to marital bliss, a "win/win" way to save face.

September 1, 1989, was going to be my last day with FedEx because I'd accepted a job elsewhere, but I was determined to get one free spouse trip. We chose the airline with the best benefits and decided we'd go wherever it went. Lake Clark National Park, along the shores of Twin Lakes, is three hundred miles west of Anchorage – over a mountain range, in a place with no roads, no normal access, and no civilization – just what we were looking for.

This is, of course, an Alaskan story. Alaskans go on vacations that other people would only call ordeals. To get to Twin Lakes, we'd have to transfer in Iliamna to another, smaller plane. We made all the arrangements and chartered our plane and pilot. I picked up Tim's to-be-validated spouse pass, and we were ready.

Unfortunately, the state of Alaska wasn't. Alaska law requires a three-day waiting period before you can get a marriage license. I had deliberated over this marriage for years, and then the state of Alaska wanted to make sure I'd really thought about it. So we rescheduled the plane, the pilot, and the nuptial vows, and on day three off we raced to the airport, lugging our duffel bags and one hundred pounds of collapsible kayak.

The journey involved a series of planes which decreased steadily in size: a Twin Otter gave way to a Cessna 185, which gave way to (I think) a Super Cub. There was no seat for me in the Cub; I had to sit on top of the bags and the hundred-pound kayak. Any of this would have been challenging enough for the woman known to Federal Express as the "Barf Queen" but the toy plane at the end was the limit.

The pilot dropped us off at Twin Lakes. That raw, empty look that thrills me still, everything windblown, barren, fighting to stay alive in the elements. Emptiness and space. It was just us, and the pilot was leaving. He would meet us there, in that exact spot, seven days later, but for now we would have this Alaska wilderness to ourselves. All these mountains, lakes, rocks, and blueberries. We couldn't sit down without staining our jeans purple. I had blueberries, Tim, and Alaska. We even found a soft, mossy spot for the tent. Wasn't marriage wonderful?

That night, while we were tucked cozily into our sleeping bags, the wind started to pick up. Our soft, mossy tent site couldn't hold onto the tent stakes, and they started lifting up. The tent sagged. Tim changed position so he could put his head downwind and the low tent ceiling wouldn't irritate him. He told me his feet would anchor the tent, and he stuck his toes up like little soldiers. I didn't think he was getting the picture. The tent was collapsing around my head.

Then the rain started. With the wind blowing from all sides, rain got in everywhere. Structurally, something was very, very wrong, but Tim still thought he was anchoring everything with his feet. It was obvious I had to take action. Cleverly, I took off my clothes. It is, after all, easier to dry skin than clothing.

I grabbed the tent and staked it down. Tim shouted congratulations from inside. But when I let go, the whole thing blew off again. I felt like the person who touches the TV antenna, the picture clears up, and everyone yells, "Stay like that!" Tim yelled, "Stay like that!" so I stayed. Wet, naked, and cold, I held on. I had this idea that if I held on long enough, it would "take." But Tim laughed just a little too much, so I marched back in the tent and handed the problem over to him. I'd had enough of the hero role. I was married.

Tim hauled the hundred-pounds-when-dry kayak bags over to the tent and staked the tent onto them. Even the winds couldn't lift those bags. That was as close as that kayak got to water and as close as we got to idyllic for the rest of the honeymoon.

In the morning, it became clear that the Mt.-McKinley-expedition-weight tent poles had bent. It was also clear that we couldn't sit in the tent forever, so Tim began building a lean-to and an elaborate pulley system to raise our food bags up into the trees and I filled everything empty with blueberries. He wanted us to eat heavy things first so the bags would be easier to raise. I wanted to eat things in containers so I could create more berry storage. There was lots of bear sign. We decided it was better to eat everything.

So did the animals. Something ate all the rubber seams in the kayak bags.

Why do Alaskans do this? We go into the mountains to get away from stress and find ourselves in a state of heart-stopping terror over bears. My huge supply of blue-berries no longer seemed so desirable. Although. . . maybe I should collect a giant amount. Then, if a bear approached, he'd eat the blueberries instead of us.

Seven days went by. The wind blew, the sun never came out. We'd sit under the lean-to, brace against the wind, and duck out just long enough to pee. When we needed to move, we went on hikes and found masses of matted down grass.

"Must have been a moose," said Tim.

"Are you sure?" I asked. "Why can't a bear do that?"

"I was trying to keep you from getting scared," Tim replied. "I can't believe we're walking through tall grass when a bear could run up on us without our even seeing him."

So we walked along the beach and the wind blew water all over us. I remember the roar of that relentless wind, the muscles it took just to sit still. I think if it had been more than seven days, we would've been marking Xs on stones.

Oh, but the pick-up. There we were, snuggled in the tent, when we heard a plane overhead. Hooray! Tim said it was our pilot, so, like crazy people, we raced around packing things, getting ready for him to circle back and pick us up. Down came the tent, the lean-to, the pulley system. Packed, orderly, and ready, we sat on the kayak bags, waiting. We were happy as clams, glad to be heading home.

We waited for three hours.

Finally, we stood up and reassembled the tent. Bent poles re-bent became broken poles. Rerun lean-tos are more like leaning-overs, and hey, with most of our food eaten, why bother lifting it into the trees? Maybe if we just hid it, the bears wouldn't find it. There's no oomph for setting up a camp twice.

But there was plenty of mental energy left for worrying. Maybe, after all, it was better not to get picked up, a plane ride in that weather could kill us. Was that really our pilot anyway? Did our real pilot forget about us? Would our friends call the pilot and remind him if we never showed? Had we told them who he was? Could we live on blueberries and fish?

I could and did keep this up for a whole day. I raised hypothetical questions and Tim refused to provide hypothetical answers. Every little sound was a plane engine until – it was our plane! And our pilot! We danced for joy. He flew round and round, but he didn't land! He flew away.

Tim and I stared at each other. Did we break camp again? Did we really want to repeat this drill? But what if he came back and we weren't ready? Where WAS he?

Tim decided that the pilot meant for us to walk further down the tundra to a place where he could land, a place where there were no whitecaps on the water. How could Tim know this was what he "meant"? When you're lost, aren't you supposed to stay where you are? But Tim was sure, and here is the amazing thing: I followed him.

We packed up and headed out. This was no walk down a sandy beach. This was tundra. Those basketballs sticking out of the surface of the earth were tussocks. Feet fall off tussocks and twist in the cracks between them. Feet have to be lifted really high to get back on tussocks again. This was miles and miles of stadium stairs with hundreds of pounds on our backs. Duffel bags aren't meant to go on backs. Duffel bags are for dropping junk from a plane and leaving in one place. Same with a hundred-pound kayak in bags that have been chewed to the point of disintegration.

How could we possibly get from here to there? And where was "there" anyway? What if the pilot was just waving, and he came back tomorrow and we weren't there because Tim thought the pilot was sending hand signals? We were in the middle of the Alaskan wilderness, but Tim chose this moment to develop tons of character defects.

This was a Marriage Moment. This was also, as Tim growled, a survival situation and no, I could not bring my gallons of blueberries. We even had to leave the kayak behind. Screw the kayak.

Screw him, too.

But I took the leap of faith. I followed my brand-new spouse (still unable to say the H-word) because he had a plan and because I didn't want to be without him. Not because I agreed with him, trusted him, or even loved him anymore. I just didn't want to be out there all alone.

I didn't go quietly. I muttered to myself. I yelled at Tim. He glowered back. Whoever was wrong on this one was GOING TO PAY, no doubt about it. The honeymoon had killed the marriage.

Three and a half miles of tortured shoulders, pinched fingers, and aching backs, three and a half miles of angry telepathic thoughts, and a mirage formed on the tundra. It was our pilot, walking towards us. I couldn't believe it, but he was there, and we were saved. Oh, we were so tough. We were a Mountain Couple, we could eat nails for breakfast. We were invincible.

We were Alaskans.

As we loaded the airplane, I discovered the gallons of blueberries.

"I knew you wanted them," my husband said.

I decided I would love him forever. He saved my life and my berries.

The pilot handed me a barf bag and said, "These winds are killers."

Oh, we made it out. Sure we had to pay the pilot to fly in again – weeks later – to pick up the kayak bags. So much for the money saved on a spouse pass. But we were really alive, and if a honeymoon doesn't make you feel glad to be alive, what's it worth after all? ✒

❧

*What had I done? I had purchased
a remote cabin in Alaska in the dead
of winter. I had taken the owner's
word that I would be able to get my
two children and myself in and out.
I had never used a wood stove.
I didn't know how to chop wood.
I was paralyzed with fear.*

Pati Crofut

Wanted:
Cheap, Waterfront Cabin

A family's wilderness lesson in self-reliance

by Pati Crofut

Like many Alaskans, Pati Crofut came to Anchorage for a summer vacation in 1981 and never went back. Pati is a self-employed accountant/trainer, writer and licensed private pilot. She is the author of *Working Parents, Happy Kids—Strategies for Staying Connected.* She is a single mom who lives with her two children ages 8 and 14, two cats, two dogs, and a cockatoo. As a family they pursue Nordic skiing, soccer and of course spending time at her cabin. She would like to dedicate this story to Quinsey, Cale and Chocolate, all her lake neighbors, and especially Wayno. ✍

No MATTER HOW BAD THINGS GOT in my marriage, I have to say my husband was a great cook. He also gave me a thirst for adventure that will never be quenched.

When I met my husband, a commercial airline pilot, I was new to Alaska. I had never flown in a little airplane, never slept in a sleeping bag, and never been out of the country. When we were deciding where to go for our honeymoon my husband-to-be said, "pick any place in the entire world." I watched as he spun the globe. Feeling very adventurous, I said, "Hawaii." Looking at me as though I hadn't understood correctly, he repeated "any place in the world." I began to understand that perhaps Hawaii wasn't exactly pushing the envelope.

We ended up going to Thailand. Fourteen countries, three children, and a multitude of Alaskan adventures later, our daughter Danny died and our marriage spiraled down quicker than an airplane in a nosedive. My grief took me into an abyss I sometimes thought had swallowed me whole. His grief took him to the bottom of the tequila bottle and the bed of a girl-friend of mine.

The divorce went through fast after I gave up worrying about who got what. I took what was offered to me: a few thousand dollars, a rag tag Zodiac boat. Using my reinstated maiden name, I signed the decree on the dotted line and started to plan the rest of my life. With my new economic status run-ning close to the poverty line, I knew I wasn't going to be flit-ting around the world any more. But once you've walked on the greener grass, it's hard to stay on your side of the fence. The question became, "just how much adventure can a few thousand dollars from a divorce settlement buy?"

I decided to look for a cook later.

Rather than searched for, I was led to my new adventure. My nighttime dreams changed from divorce courtroom drama to a recurring dream of a little brown cabin in the woods. So frequent was this dream, I found the vision invading my day-time thoughts.

I was pulled by this image and the peace it promised me. In January, the month my daughter Quinsey turned three, I placed an ad in the local newspaper.

WANTED — CHEAP, WATERFRONT CABIN
REMOTE, YET ACCESSIBLE, CLOSE TO ANCHORAGE

I fielded the phone calls, looked at a few cabins, took names, and followed up on other leads. One month later a woman called me. She knew of a cabin that was going up for sale. I called Vigo, the owner, and one night later my children and I were in his living room watching a video he had filmed of the cabin. It was a good-sized cabin with a loft, located on East Butterfly Lake on the Nancy Lake Canoe Trail System. It had an artesian well and an outdoor hot tub heated by a wood stove. No jet skis, no powerboats.

"How do I get there?" I asked.

"In the summer, you drive sixty-seven miles out on the Parks Highway, drive eight miles down a four-wheel drive road, hike two miles, paddle across the lake and you're home. Three hours, door-to-door," Vigo said. "In the winter, you snow machine ten miles over a winter trail." He then offered to take my eight-year-old son Cale and I out to see it the next weekend.

We met at the Nancy Lake Marina and snow machined ten miles in to the cabin. Before he even opened the front door, I knew this was the cabin from my dream. While waiting for the woodstove to take some of the chill out of the minus-20 air inside the cabin, Cale and I looked around. We both spotted the bear head at once.

"I'm sure there's a story to that one," I said.

"It seems," he said, "that this cabin might be on a bear trail because it gets broken into more often than the others on the lake." He then showed me the four gaping holes in each corner of the cabin. They were boarded up on the outside. "Well," he added, "I may as well show you the couch, too." We pulled the couch away from the wall and saw that the bear had literally eaten the back of it.

Vigo looked at me and said, "You know, this scenario was one that my wife and I never entertained. A single woman with two small kids was just not who we thought would end up with this cabin. Part of me is disappointed because I don't think you're going to be real impressed with my tool shed and with all the tools that come with this cabin. But this is a great cabin, and the neighbors on this lake are a great bunch of people."

The money changed hands, maintenance of the cabin was explained, and I became the new owner. I called and introduced myself to all my new neighbors on the lake and made arrangements to hike in with one of them when the four-wheel drive road became passable towards the end of May.

In the weeks between winter and May, I would wake up in the middle of the night in a cold sweat. What had I done? I had purchased a remote cabin in Alaska in the dead of winter. I had taken the owner's word that I would be able to get my two children and myself in and out. I had never used a wood stove. I didn't know how to chop wood. I was paralyzed with fear.

Although, by this time, I had had a lot of experience backpacking, I overpacked in my zeal to have everything the three of us would need to eat well and have fun. Luckily, my daughter Quinsey was a peanut of a child weighing less than thirty pounds. Yet after loading her into my pack along with our rain gear, extra clothes, food and first aid kit, I knew better than to weigh the final load.

As it turned out, ignorance was not bliss. When we met my new lake neighbor, Wayno, at the trailhead and started on our hike, I'm sure he eyed my load with dread thinking he'd be carrying some of it by the end of the hike. Wayno is the modern day Alaskan man. A certified public accountant during the week, he transforms into the rugged outdoorsman on weekends. Another Swede like Vigo and a Minnesota transplant, he is able to fix anything with or without tools and parts. He is full of facts and stories about animal behavior and is always ready to help out a neighbor. If Wayno says that something can't be done, end of story.

Maybe I'm just stubborn. Maybe it's the Irish stoic in me. Maybe I just wanted my children to go into this venture feeling they could depend on me. With the words to Mick Jagger's "Beast of Burden" echoing through my mind, I made it to the end of the trail without help, vowing to lighten the load next time.

The trail is a rolling narrow four-wheel drive road that weaves between three lakes and through two bogs. The vegetation changes dramatically from week to week, leading off with the fiddlehead ferns in May and ending with the devil's club dressed in a brilliant yellow in October. In four years I have seen the bogs dry only once. Most of the time they are oozing with thick, deep muck. There is no way to reach my cabin with dry feet. All of us fell in the bog on this first hike. Once in, the weight of my pack made it impossible for me to get back out. Wayno extended his hand, and I was up and out. Sitting in my pack as I went in and out of the bog, Quinsey thought it was fun.

As we peaked the last hill of the hike, the lake revealed itself sparkling through the trees. The trail ends on the opposite side of the lake from our cabin. To climb into a small boat and putt across the lake to the cabin, after driving and hiking, is a certain stress reliever. The kids leaned back on the rubber of the Zodiac with their faces welcoming the breeze. Our dog Chocolate laid on the bottom of the boat in his own doggy bliss.

We spent the first weekend checking things out. The kids slept in different places each night, and sat in different chairs each day. The cabin was so well-equipped and well-organized that I quickly realized it would be a while before it started to feel like our cabin instead of Vigo's.

Our first night in the cabin the skies opened up. Sheets of rain enveloped our dwelling. There was no getting out and we knew no one was coming to visit. I have never felt so safe and protected. We pulled out the sofa bed, made a small fire in the wood stove, and got under the blankets with Chocolate. We slept like we were drugged.

The rest of the weekend was spent learning cabin chores and choosing the roles we would assume at our weekend retreat. Cale picked up the axe and learned to split wood. We experimented with the hot tub. The first soak was a chiller, because although the thermometer read 100 degrees, we had neglected to stir the water as it heated. It was 100 degrees at the top of the tub while the bottom was a refreshing 40 degrees. Four years later we are able to inch the temperature up to 102 degrees and keep it hovering there for hours while we soak in the hot tub and dip in the lake, or the snow, depending on the season.

Wayno became our hiking companion. As it turned out we were both retreating to the woods that summer. He was on the verge of a divorce, so each weekend we would hightail it out of Anchorage, meet at the trailhead and walk in together. We would arrange a time to leave at the end of the weekend and then walk back out together. He welcomed us as hiking companions through black bear country and remarked more than once that my children's constant chatter was better bear protection than the pepper spray I carried on my belt.

The bears struck about the third week in June that first summer. I had warning. My lake neighbor Ray went in mid-week and called to tell me about the break-in. Friends over the years have related dramatic stories of bears breaking into cabins. They peppered each account with vivid descriptions of the bears destroying everything and leaving their signatures by urinating or defecating all over the inside of these cabins.

With these images in our minds, Cale, Quinsey and I were both surprised and pleased by what we found. The bear had entered by pulling off the siding to the right of the door. Yes, the food was gone — all of it. And yes, there was a claw hole poked through every container — dish soap, shampoo, tooth paste, cleaning agents, crayon boxes and board games. We could easily discern the path of the bear by following the trail of bear hairs over the floor, on top of the counters and through the pantry. We had to smile at the perfect paw prints he left by smearing the lemonade and hot chocolate powder. The entire fifty-pound sack of dog food was gone. But nothing was broken, and Mr. Bear did not "mark" our cabin. He simply ate and ran.

Cleanup was surprisingly quick. In order to avoid further break-ins we decided not to keep any food in the cabin. "Pack it in and pack it out" became our motto. We nixed the idea of carrying a gun. I don't like them, and I don't know how to use one anyway. My friend Beth says that having a gun is like caring for an infant. You have to take care of it. You have to know where it is at all times. I'm taking care of two kids already. We decided to battle the bears with our brains.

Bear lectures suggested an arsenal of weapons in addition to guns: ammonia, mothballs, solar-powered electric wires, boards with nails sticking out of them, flare guns, firecrackers, pepper spray. Our weapons of choice became ammonia, mothballs, and pepper spray. We anointed our cabin with ammonia around the perimeter and little piles of mothballs in each of the corners where the break-ins always occurred.

Together, we made our plan of defense. In case of bear attack, Chocolate would sound the early warning inside the cabin. After all, I figured, he is a Bernese Mountain dog and providing protection is one of the traits of this breed. We would quickly locate the point of entry. Cale would stand ready with the axe to knock the bear on the head as he poked through the wall. I would then spray him with pepper spray. Quinsey would run out the door and club him on his butt. It sounded plausible to all of us. We slept like babies with our weapons nearby. We were a unit, and we were invincible.

In facing the bears, we faced ourselves. We learned to trust and rely on one another. We acquired backcountry skills simply by being there. As things broke we figured out how to fix them. Any idea was a good idea if it worked. There was no calling a repairperson up on the phone, or getting in the car to go looking for a repair part.

As we encountered wildlife on the trail, or at the cabin, we identified them later by looking them up in books or asking the Fish and Game. Our most magical animal encounter was the time we all walked out of the cabin and saw our rolled-up living room rug dancing on top of the woodpile. I had tossed it there after ripping it out of the cabin. Upon closer inspection we spotted small, furry brown and white critters with huge ears and wide eyes all over the woodpile and inside the rug. Quinsey screamed in delight wanting to hold one of them. Later we found out they were ermine. The next weekend we were disappointed to find they had moved on.

We also have a family of beavers. It looked as though they were going to build a new lodge right in front of our cabin last summer. Many nights we would lie on the deck at dusk and watch them at work less than ten feet away. They cleared out an area of trees and then moved further down the lake. One of the trees that the beavers had been working on began to lean towards the hot tub. Fearing that our soaks and facials were in serious danger, my friend Catherine and I decided to cut it down. She said all we had to do was attach a rope around the tree and pull on it to guide the tree where we wanted it to fall, while the other person worked the chainsaw. I had never operated a chainsaw or cut a tree down, but Catherine is an architect and a graduate of Yale. If she said this was going to work, I saw no reason to wait around. Designing houses, cutting trees — there's an overlap of skills here, I reasoned.

As the chainsaw ate its way through the trunk of the tree we were surprised to find out how heavy that tree was and that we were not going to be guiding it anywhere. "Get out of the way!" we screamed at our five children standing on the dock as the tree headed straight for them. The kids leaped into the water, the dock was dented, but the hot tub survived.

A flock of ptarmigans took refuge in our shed one year. We recreated a scene from The Birds when we flung the shed doors open. The haunting, plaintive cries of the loons used to send Quinsey beneath the blankets. Cale and I could say nothing to calm her fears. Now, having observed their mating dance and their babies over the last four years, she has acquired an appreciation and love for them.

The bears continue to break into our cabin. So much for the mothballs and ammonia. I sided the back of the cabin with metal, and what seemed like 40,000 screws and the bears zeroed in on the front. The entire cabin has metal siding on it now. Each summer everyone on our lake anxiously waits to see what the bears will do with the new deterrents. It is a perpetual science experiment. Mercury, my neighbor on the other side, is fearful that if I am successful in building a bear-proof fortress, the bears will be so angry they will migrate next door and trash his cabin.

While I deal with bears, Mercury is dealing with squirrels. Refusing to poison or shoot them, he experiments weekly with live-catch traps and sealing off yet another opening in his cabin.

He and Wayno had breakfast one morning, and the ceiling came down in their cereal bowls. The squirrels had gnawed away a good portion of the ceiling. We fear that soon Mercury will be sitting at his table with nothing but a shell around him.

Last summer, I got the mid-week call again. But this time it was human vandals that attacked. Shooting out windows and kicking in doors, they went from cabin to cabin stealing alcohol and guns. When Wayno left a message on my phone telling me to bring a door into the cabin, I knew my carpentry skills were about to be tested. I sought the advice of my friend Ben. Hanging out at his construction job site, I was able to steer him away from his job to give me lessons in doorknob installation.

Armed with a Makita drill and battery pack, we hiked in to make the repairs. After spending hours fiddling with the tools, the parts and lining up the door jam hole, I now have a personal relationship with "my" doorknob. I can't help but fondle it each time I go in or out of the cabin.

I found our cabin to be the perfect litmus test for male relationships. I was in a rut with three Daves in a row, all of them engineers. Dave Number One dumped me and the kids into the lake in the middle of May as he got into our canoe. In the dead of winter, Dave Number Two set his alarm clock to go off every two hours. He felt that continually feeding the woodstove was more important than sleeping. Dave Number Three watched while Cale, Quinsey and I did all the cabin chores. All the Daves had this obsession with the cabin fire detector. Dave Number One thought the best place for it was on the wall downstairs. Dave Number Two remarked on what a ridiculous place that was and moved it upstairs to the loft. As Dave Number Three entered our cabin, we cut to the chase and asked him where he wanted to reinstall the fire detector. He thought the perfect place for it was right above the woodstove. Maybe moving fire detectors is a man's way of marking his territory.

But, many weekends on East Butterfly Lake, it is just me and my two kids. It is hard to describe the solitude of the wilderness. Being alone and unobserved is a little like singing in the shower. In our first weekends alone we might run out onto the dock and sing as loud as we could. Or I would read loudly from Emerson while the kids booed and hissed. Once we mooned the loons. We have also been known to indulge in skinny dipping now and then, and some nights we can be seen dancing in the dusk on our deck. Or we get up on three wooden tables, turn on reggae music and boogie like Rastafarians. My friend Trisha spent an entire weekend trying to teach Cale how to move his hips while keeping his knees together. Sometimes, late in the evening, we'll take the "harbor cruise" and paddle the canoe around the lake checking on our little piece of paradise and all of the creatures in it.

Each winter we charter in with a flight service and stay the week over New Year's. The pilots always wince when we arrive for our flight with skis, snowshoes, lots of food, outdoor gear and an eighty-five pound dog. Temperatures of minus 20 are not unusual. The woodstove is plenty big enough to keep the cabin cozy. We keep the hot tub running most of the time. Instead of dips in the lake, the kids go from the hot tub to the snow. Or we all sit in the tub and count while someone gets out of the tub and runs barefoot onto the lake. No one has made it past the count of 33.

We replaced the rubber Zodiac with a metal boat named "The Beast." The bears were constantly poking holes in the rubber of the "Zode," and the beavers ate our oars. Too often we would hike to the end of the trail only to find a deflated boat. After pumping it up, Cale would have to hold his finger over the hole, while we motored across the lake as fast as we could.

Cabin plans for another New Year are underway. We realize we are no longer getting over the divorce or Danny's death. We've gone through to the other side. We have photo albums and guest books inside the cabin overflowing with wonderful memories. Quinsey is eight and now walks into the cabin carrying a small pack. Cale is fourteen and stronger than I am now. Chocolate is getting older, but he is still our "pointman" for bear entries. Mack is our new family member, a Yukon River Husky we rescued from the pound as he was taking his "final death walk." Wayno met and married a woman named Katie, and Mercury is dating Wayno's ex-wife.

And me? Well, I've sworn off engineers, but I'm still looking for a good cook. ⋖

❦

Takput decided to take a
shortcut and not the much-traveled
seventy-five mile ice road along
the frozen edge of the Beaufort Sea.
The shortcut was just a trail, not
often plowed, and snaked for many
miles across the frozen tundra.

Marilyn Forrester

The Blizzard

How to get a teaching job in the Alaskan Bush

by Marilyn Forrester

Marilyn Forrester arrived in Anchorage, newly divorced, with $200 and her return ticket—planning to "just look around." After 22 years in Alaska, she is still "looking around." She went to work for Alyeska Pipeline Service Company, first in Anchorage, then at Pump Station 5, and later at Prudhoe Bay. While working at Prudhoe Bay she was persuaded to apply for a position at Alaska Business College. She was hired over the phone and, to her surprise, found that she liked teaching. Going back to school, she received two more degrees and a Masters. Her first job was teaching in Napaskiak, Alaska, and after that she taught in Barrow, Kotzebue, Nondalton, Nuiqsut, and Tok. She also spent a year as a teacher in Kekaha, Kauai. She is now semi-retired and working on a book relating her ten years of teaching experiences in the Alaska Bush. ⤝

"WE HAVE TO GET ON THE MAIL PLANE," said my friend Roger, a young kindergarten teacher who had that day learned he would not be offered a new contract.

It was April, and we were in my classroom in Nuiqsut, a small Eskimo village about one hundred thirty-six miles east of Barrow. My term replacing a first grade teacher on sick leave was about to end, and I needed one more year for retirement. We needed to get to Anchorage for the Teacher Job Fair to find teaching positions for the next year. As any teacher who attends these job fairs knows, the first day is the most important. I was sure that if I couldn't get there by the first day, my chances of finding a job were slim. The superintendents check only those resumes collected on the beginning day.

The village, one of three abandoned villages resettled in 1973 by twenty-seven families from Barrow, is home to nearly five hundred residents. Trapper School, where we taught, had only one hundred forty-eight students. The area is known as "The Top of the World" because of its proximity to the North Pole. Over ninety percent of the residents are Inupiat Eskimos who live a subsistence lifestyle, hunting, fishing, and whaling.

In anticipation of an approaching blizzard, the airline grounded the regular plane. When I called to reserve seats on the mail plane, the lady told me, "We have two extra seats, but you can only take twenty pounds of luggage."

"My makeup alone weighs that much," I said.

It didn't matter. They grounded the mail plane, too.

Takput, an Inupiat Eskimo whose son was in my first grade class, heard of our plight and, needing the money, came to the school. In his thirties, he wore his wolf parka, beaver hat, and fur mukluks with ease.

"I want to try it out," he said, as he pointed proudly to his new, bright blue truck. "If you will pay me the same as the plane fare, I will bring you to Prudhoe to catch the plane to Anchorage."

Knowing that the Prudhoe plane for Anchorage left at eight o'clock in the evening, we jumped at Takput's offer. This was a chance to get our extra household and teaching supplies to Anchorage without having to pay to ship them at the end of the year. I took my stereo and four large boxes. Roger loaded his extra supplies into the truck, and we started out for Prudhoe Bay at four that afternoon.

Extreme winter conditions are common on the North Slope and, with the wind chill, the temperatures often drop to minus one hundred degrees Fahrenheit. On average, we spent two hundred ninety-seven days a year in below-freezing weather. As I trudged to school in my heavy winter clothing, I often saw foxes and wolves.

The North Slope of Alaska has over two months of complete darkness each winter. One January the principal insisted that everyone go outside for the year's first sunrise. It was eighty below and my first graders were cold. The children were singing songs to the new sun that would soon appear. They had sparklers and were stamping their feet to keep warm. Some were crying and the twins in my class got too close to the sparklers and set their coats on fire. We put the fires out quickly with snow and no one was injured. Everyone was happy when we were allowed to go inside. The event was supposed to be recorded on film but it was too cold for the camera to work. After that experience, we watched from inside for the sun to appear. I was always happy to see the first day of sunshine as it meant that the long winter was almost over. During the months of darkness, I felt like a mole living underground.

In 1977 I arrived in Anchorage with my return ticket to Laguna Beach, California, and two hundred dollars to spend. I told everyone that I wasn't staying, that I had only come to look around. Here I was, twenty years later, still "looking around." Sometimes as I trudged through the snow in a Nuiqsut blizzard on a dark morning and heading for the school, I would ask myself, "What are you doing here? You hate snow and detest cold weather. Have you lost your mind?"

In spite of the difficulties of Bush living, though, I loved Alaska and teaching the Native children. I had come to Alaska to get rich, but now I was staying because Alaska was my home.

Roger had been teaching in Little Diomede, across from Siberia, and was familiar with the darkness, climate, and lack of personal conveniences. He considered Nuiqsut "the city."

Although he was young and had only been teaching for a few years, he was an imaginative and creative teacher. The children loved him, and he was full of enthusiasm.

We hurriedly completed lesson plans, found substitute teachers for our classes, and packed our belongings. When we started, the snow was already falling and the temperature was fifty degrees below zero.

Takput decided to take a shortcut and not the much-traveled seventy-five mile ice road along the frozen edge of the Beaufort Sea. By ice road you can reach Deadhorse, the Prudhoe Bay airport, in two hours. The shortcut was just a trail, not often plowed, and snaked for many miles across the frozen tundra. Although shorter, few people travel it because of the danger in getting lost.

When the blizzard hit, we could not see anything but snow. We had gone about five miles when we slid down a small slope into our first ditch. I was in a panic that we would never get to Prudhoe Bay to catch the plane, and that we would freeze to death, lost on the frozen tundra.

Safety experts tell you not to travel without a second vehicle to accompany you, have a good radio, wear ski pants, and bring extra food. We did. When we tried to radio for help, we only got static. Our jeans froze to our legs as we pushed the truck. The snow was falling so thickly that I could barely see Roger. I lost all contact with my ears and my mittened hands were numb. My feet were frozen blocks of ice. When I jumped up and down to get my feet warm, needles of pain shot through my legs.

Each time I got back into the truck to get warm, it would go a few yards and then into the ravine on the other side. There wasn't any visible road and after pushing the truck out several times, Takput said, "You two walk ahead. Keep me on road."

We couldn't see our feet. It was like being in a tunnel without an end. Soon we lost all sense of which way to turn. Roger took my hand. I was glad.

The wet snow hit my frozen face and swirled to the ground. I heard the wind howling over the miles of frigid tundra. "You are not going to make it," I thought. "Next time we won't be able get the truck out. You haven't got food or warm clothing. They will find all of you in the spring when the snow melts, and your body will be chewed on by polar bears. Then your California friends will say, 'Whatever was she doing up there in that God-forsaken place?'"

Roger looked at me and asked, "Are you crying?"

Brushing some moisture from my eyes, I said, "Not yet." But it was a struggle not to just sit down in a snow bank and weep.

Roger said, "Well, at least we won't freeze to death because I have a lot of heirloom quilts in one box." I wasn't only worried about freezing. All I could think about were polar bears charging us. Their white teeth gleaming, they would be on top of me before I knew what hit me, their thousand-pound bodies crushing me into the snow. I imagined their keen sense of smell identifying us as food more than ten miles away and running towards us at thirty-five miles an hour. I remembered what I had learned about these animals. Polar bears do not hibernate, have very sharp teeth, and stalk before they pounce.

Many hours later, we finally saw lights up ahead. We had found the ice road! Our truck slid into another ditch, and this time we couldn't push it out. Roger and I got out and tried to put something under the wheels. There wasn't anything available so we used snow.

Takput sat in the truck. His only contribution was to offer us some peanuts. Roger and I shook our heads. We were not interested in peanuts.

After what seemed like an eternity, we spotted a Prudhoe Bay driver lumbering along in a large rolligon, a 52,000-pound metal caterpillar with eight airbags for tires. Roger, Takput, and I jumped out and began waving our arms, yelling as loudly as we could. The rolligon driver shouted from his window, "Have you any rope?"

Of course not.

The driver rumbled off to find some rope. I was afraid that he wouldn't return but Roger told me, "Don't worry, Marilyn. He'll be back soon, and then we'll be on our way. Tonight we'll have a nice dinner at Prudhoe Bay and catch the first plane in the morning for Anchorage. It'll be okay."

Takput was quiet. A two-hour trip had turned into an eight-hour ordeal, and the Anchorage plane had gone without us.

After what felt like a lifetime, the rolligon driver returned with a rope and pulled us out of the ditch. We got to the Prudhoe Bay Inn at midnight. The hotel was an ATCO trailer and dark when we arrived. The dim lobby had one person behind the desk and a small desk lamp was all that lit the interior.

An old, whiskered man woke from his snoring and shuffled toward the desk. We signed the book and he gave us each a key, pointing down the long dark hallway.

"I am sorry that you missed your plane," was all Takput said. But he still took our eighty dollars.

Since we weren't going to get anything to eat because the dining room was closed, Roger and I mumbled good night and staggered down the narrow hallway to our rooms.

My one hundred twenty-five-dollar a night room didn't have hangers, telephone, TV, clock, or towels. Hungry and tired, I wanted to shower. Not finding one in my room, I decided that perhaps there was a community shower. Maybe the towels and soap would also be there.

At the end of the darkened corridor, I found a large room with many shower stalls separated by curtains. It was spooky and empty at that hour of the night. I managed to locate a tiny piece of soap but no towels. Dripping water on the wooden floor, I finally found a box of tissues. I dried myself as well as I could with little pieces of tissue sticking here and there to my skin.

The next morning we took the first plane into Anchorage, and I rushed to the Captain Cook Hotel for the Teachers' Job Fair straight from the airport. Other female teachers were tripping around with briefcases and high heels, but I charged in in parka and fur boots, résumé in hand.

After all we had been through, Roger decided to just party and see if he could get the principal to relent when he returned to the village. That is exactly what happened. We laugh about our adventure every time we bump into each other in Anchorage.

I told the first interviewer about my ordeal and said, "Don't you think I deserve a job after all I have been through?" The news of my adventure traveled quickly. Soon other district representatives clamored to interview me.

One superintendent asked me to meet his School Board. After the interview, they requested that I tell my story one more time. When I came to the part about showering and drying with tissues, one School Board member said, "You are a real Bush teacher, and we are going to hire you."

And they did. ᐊᕗ

❧

I have lived with moose all my life. Moose in Anchorage are like pigeons in Boston, only bigger. When I cross-country ski, moose are usually lurking in the woods next to the trails. Unlike encounters with bears, meeting moose in the woods doesn't conjure up grisly scenes in my head.

Karen L. Heath

Bullwinkle's Evil Cousin

A close encounter of the moose kind

by Karen L. Heath

Karen L. Heath lives in Anchorage with her husband, three kids, and two dogs—all unruly. A lifelong Alaskan, she tried living in the Lower 48 but returned after five years. With a Masters in Vocational Rehabilitation, her husband wonders when she'll find a real job. She has written for *Alaska Parenting*, *Ruralite*, and *Horizons*. ❧

THE MOOSE STOOD just off the trail, benignly eating some willows. The muscles in her shoulders rippled as she turned her head to look at us, her brown ears twitching slightly. We made eye contact. The dogs saw her. We started past her, assessing her tension, her actions, her nerves, her ears. Nothing in her demeanor prepared me for what happened next. Head down, ears back, she charged.

Only moments before I had been skiing down the trail under dog power, what the Norwegians call skijoring. Held to my two dogs by a long bungee-like rope which was attached to the skijor belt around my waist, my skis bumped lightly over the snow. I clenched my toes to keep my balance. Blanca's red tail curled up like a swirled lollipop, and she trotted, barely pulling against her red harness. Winter, her white tail tucked under, curved her body into the purple harness, straining from the weight of me. Blanca wasn't pulling much weight, but it seemed she and Winter had made a deal: Winter would pull, and Blanca would interpret my commands. I pushed hard with my poles, resting my arms intermittently. Blanca would turn accusingly when I stopped poling, wondering why her load had increased.

The dogs' tongues dangled out the side of their mouths. A rush of exercise-induced euphoria surged through my body. Life was good.

Up the trail I saw a man walking his two bulky Siberian huskies. My lean, fast sled dogs looked small and weak compared to his powerful dogs.

"On by. On by Blanca. On by Winter! ON BY!" I yelled, giving them the command to keep going. Blanca often veers off, sniffing at the dogs we're passing, so I rarely make eye contact with other dog owners. I watched Blanca to make sure she went straight past. This time she only leaned a little, and I praised her vigorously. Winter, my fraidy-cat, rarely veers off. The man's dogs struggled against their leashes as we passed. He yelled something, and I turned my head to hear him better.

"There's a moose about two hundred yards up."

"OK, thanks," I yelled back.

It was decision time. Turn around and pass the two dogs again, more difficult for the owner of the two Siberians and me because we would be going in the same direction, or ski up and see if the moose was still there. I decided on the latter, convinced I would have time to turn back if the moose was standing in the middle of the trail. I was challenging myself, as sometimes I thought I was too cautious.

I saw the moose off the trail shortly before the dogs did. Snowplowing, I slowed to a stop. "Whoa, girls."

Winter, although nervous around other dogs, loves to chase moose, so I watched her. It seemed for the moment that her love of pulling was overpowering her love of harassing moose. I watched the moose for signs of agitation. Her ears twitched, but I'd seen that many times in the moose that bed down in my backyard in the winter, or come in the fall to strip the leaves off my raspberry bushes.

I have lived with moose all my life. Moose in Anchorage are like pigeons in Boston, only bigger. When I cross-country ski, moose are usually lurking in the woods next to the trails. Unlike encounters with bears, meeting moose in the woods doesn't conjure up grisly death scenes in my head.

So I was shocked when I found myself the target of a charging moose. Instinctively, I aimed my skis away from her and skied into more trouble, directly into the deep snow at the trail's edge. The snow grabbed my skis, sucking me down and toppling me over. I floundered.

Menacing brown eyes stared at me down a bulbous snout. Her steaming breath reached mine. I leaned my body away from her, my right side sinking further into the snow. I couldn't take my eyes off her face. My two huskies shrunk under her stare, their tails tucked under their bodies, leaning into the snow like me. She loomed over us, her large ears back and twitching. Coarse hair between her shoulders shot straight up and she stood tall, like my huskies do when they feel threatened. Glancing at her muscular front legs, knowing long legs like those have killed people, I did what any intelligent person in the same situation would do. I started to scream.

This is not exactly what I had advised in an article I wrote for <u>Alaska Parenting</u> on moose safety. "Remain calm and hide behind a tree or some other large object," I had said. Nowhere had I mentioned screaming as an effective method to avoid confrontation with an angry moose.

I clawed at the snow for the panic release clasp that would disengage me from the dogs. Then, just as I yanked on the strap to release the dogs, the moose started a slow turn away from us. Bullwinkle's evil cousin ran crazily down the trail, her long brown legs pumping wildly. In hot pursuit were my two errant dogs who, just moments before, had been melting under her stare.

Swallowing sobs, I stood. People got in trouble with large wild animals because they made stupid mistakes. I couldn't figure out my mistake. Should I have turned around? Should I not have stopped? Was the moose just having a bad day? My shaky legs barely held me. I thought of the danger in which I had put other travelers, specifically the man we passed.

The moose swerved and dashed across the road that ran beside the trail. She was headed for deep snow where her long legs would have the advantage. Winter and Blanca yipped and yowled, their skijor rope tangled around some brush in the woods.

"Winter, Blanca, COME, COME ON girls," I yelled in vain.

They turned to me, grinning that stupid dog grin that meant they had no intention of obeying. There was a moose to chase. I took off my skis and dragged them through the deep snow towards my dogs. I made my way slowly, anxious that the moose might be lurking nearby, ready to charge again.

As I approached them, a final tug on the rope extricated them from the willows and they tore across the road. I burst from the trees onto the road. The dogs were gone, my life had just been threatened, and I felt totally alone. I took deep breaths to keep from bawling.

I looked down the road and saw two women dressed in bright yellow jogging clothes, crossing to the other side of the road. Briefly I thought maybe they were trying to avoid me, the hysterical woman who had just erupted from the woods with a wild look in her eye. I crossed to their side, the side where my dogs had gone.

"Do you have a cell phone?" I asked, panic in my voice. I was not really clear why I wanted a cell phone, but it seemed like the thing to ask for in this situation.

"No." They looked me over. "Are you all right?" one of them asked me hesitantly.

"I was just charged by a moose," I said, my tongue sticky and thick with fear. I felt like I was speaking in slow motion. The two women appeared to me as a yellow mass, not distinct from one another.

"Are you OK?" one voice asked again.

"Yeah," I said, thinking about it, unable to focus on them. I ran my hands over my body. Physically I checked out fine, but emotionally I was a mess. "Why did she charge me? Why me? I wasn't doing anything wrong. I wasn't going to hurt her. She didn't have a calf. Oh God why me? My dogs weren't after her."

The two women stared at me quietly, pity in their eyes.

"I need to find my dogs," I said. "They ran after the moose." I wanted to call my husband and have him rescue me.

"We'll go get our car," one of the yellow women told me. "What do your dogs look like?" she added.

"Alaska huskies, white, red. They are pulling a long rope behind them."

I jammed my skis into the snow on the side of the road. "I'm leaving my skis here, so you'll know where I went in," I said, thinking clearly for the first time. I watched their yellow suits bobbing down the road. I was alone again.

I headed into the woods. There were two tracks to follow: shallow dog tracks with a perfect line in the snow, like something was chasing them, and deep moose tracks. Hoping the dogs' rope would get stuck to slow them down, I waded into the tracks. Knee-deep snow covered my legs with each step, and I called, "Blanca, Winter, come on girls." Every few steps I called again. I looked for trees to duck behind in case the moose came tearing through the woods. I noted landmarks in case I got lost. An eagle's nest sat in the crook of a tall spruce's branches.

My legs and feet were numb from wading through thigh-high snow. With the eagle's nest for my landmark, I focused on survival and finding my wayward dogs. After what seemed like hours, hopelessness and sadness mixed with love and anger at my stupid dogs. I couldn't stand to think that something had happened to them. Stories of moose stomping dogs are common. I gulped big gasps of air and yelled without conviction. As I approached the road, I heard the yellow-suited women yelling back, "We've got your dogs."

Jubilant, I tried to run through the deep snow, but my legs weren't working right. My chest heaving, I scurried up the steep embankment, losing ground on the slippery slope.

Blanca and Winter were there, wagging their tails, looking perky and happy. I hugged them vigorously, burying my face in their wet, soft fur. They smelled musty, like they do after a good run.

"They were just running down the side of the road, and when we called them, they jumped right into the car," one of the joggers told me. I thought briefly that if they had been my kids, I would have scolded them for hopping so willingly into a stranger's car.

I laughed. "Heading back to my car, I bet." *Total geographical recall.* That was what a musher relative told me about Alaska huskies. I rely on them to lead the way, but this time I didn't trust them to find the car again. I should have.

One woman offered me a ride back to my car. I hesitated, then said, "No thanks." She looked at me like I was crazy. "OK, sure," I said, loading the wet dogs and my skis into her car. Blanca climbed over the seats to sit on my lap, leaving a trail of wet hair in the car. I was embarrassed and apologetic but the woman assured me it was OK.

I thanked her profusely, telling her I would help some hysterical woman next time in repayment for her kindness. We exchanged names, though I have no recollection of her face or name now, just her yellow suit and helpfulness.

"Have you lived here long?" she asked me as we drove the short distance back to my car.

I realized from her question that she was assessing my inexperience and evaluating why it happened to me. Alaskans do this, thinking if they can figure out why somebody else was put in a dangerous situation, they can avoid it, or just put it down to inexperience. I do it all the time. I'll think, after reading about a bear mauling, well, that person wasn't from here, or she did all the wrong things. Now I think I've been too harsh on those victims. They probably thought they were doing all the right things.

"All my life," I said. I felt strangely smug, relieved that I was not lying in an ambulance like the woman charged last year, or in a coffin like the blind man who was stomped to death at the University. I felt like a cat with nine lives.

"You could have been killed," the woman said.

"Yes," I said. But I wasn't. ✍

❧

My husband had lured me to
Anchorage with tales of a city
near the ocean, a place free of
snakes and natural disasters.
During the previous five years
we had been through a hurricane,
floods, numerous tornado
warnings, and thunderstorms,
so the idea of a state with no
disasters was appealing.

Molly G. Heath

How Do You Pack for an Earthquake?

Riding out the Great Alaska Earthquake of 1964

by Molly A. Heath

Molly Heath and her husband, after living almost thirty years in Alaska, returned to Texas again to face the tornadoes and thunderstorms. Their adult children and nine grandchildren still reside in Alaska, so their summers are spent in that great state, with the remainder of the year spent traveling and restoring their turn-of-the-century home. ✑

I WAS WATCHING SHADOWS DANCE on the snow-covered mountains when I detected an odd movement to our car. "Could we have a flat?"

My husband, Bob, pulled to the side of the road as the car began shaking violently. Our children were screaming with delight at the wild movement. "My God," Bob shouted,"we have four flats!"

He braked to a stop. The car continued to gyrate as if possessed. "Good God, we're in the middle of the mother of all earthquakes!" We heard a deep rumble. The slopes that had been so tranquil only moments before changed into huge menacing mounds of snow barreling down the mountainside.

The car continued to rock so hard our three kids, who were being flung from side to side in the back seat, thought it was exciting as a carnival ride.

This trip had begun so well. Bob's boss at Anchorage Natural Gas had lent us his cabin on Kenai Lake for the long Easter weekend and we were looking forward to getting away. Bob had been working six days a week and the children rarely got to see him as he usually got home after they were in bed. At last we'd cleared some time for our family to spend together, to get to know each other again.

We had moved to Alaska eighteen months before, on September 1, 1962, leaving behind a Texas heat wave of 110 degrees. Alaska was experiencing a beautiful warm fall that year with temperatures rising to sixty in the daytime and falling into the forties at night. Everyone kept telling me how warm it was, but for this Texas-born girl, it was winter.

My husband had lured me to Anchorage with tales of a city near the ocean, a place free of snakes and natural disasters. During the previous five years we had been through a hurricane, floods, numerous tornado warnings, and thunderstorms, so the idea of a state with no disasters was appealing. He forgot to mention earthquakes.

After the car finally stopped shaking, I turned to Bob. "Didn't that one seem to go on for a really long time and wasn't it a lot stronger than we've felt before?"

He shrugged "Maybe it was stronger because we're in the mountains."

Trouble started when a few miles later we came upon a huge avalanche across the road. "Well, we're not going that way," Bob said as he turned the car around and headed back to Anchorage. I swallowed the lump in my throat and tried not to cry. I had been looking forward to this time away, and now we were going back home and Bob would be called back to work. We drove in silence, each of us lost in our own worlds.

The kids were trying to recreate the earthquake by bouncing around in the back seat. At least for them, the earthquake had added excitement to an otherwise dull road trip. Three-year-old Valerie, who thought her daddy could do anything, chirped from the back seat, "Daddy, please make the car jump again. Pleeease."

Karen, who as the youngest always had to get in a word or two chimed in on the "Pleeease," but their six-year-old brother Bill remained superior and told them, "Dad can't make earthquakes happen. Only babies would think that!"

Great, all I needed was a backseat full of squabbling kids, a husband whose knuckles were white from gripping the steering wheel, and me trying to put a good face on things while quaking inside.

There were a few small avalanches on the road and we negotiated them with little difficulty, but the Placer River bridge was a mass of crumpled concrete, totally impassable by automobile. The Placer is the first of several rivers crossing the Seward Highway between the mountains and Anchorage. It is never a pretty river as it is constantly roiled by tides from Turnagain Arm. Now it was even muddier and more turbulent.

My husband cursed under his breath. "I noticed a highway camp back a ways. Maybe there are people there this weekend. At least it will be a place to get out of the cold."

In 1964, we could be assured that there would be no locks to keep us out of the buildings. Alaska was a frontier state full of people willing to help. Wilderness cabins were left unlocked with the unwritten proviso that one replaced what one used.

We had plenty of food and several five-gallon jugs of water, so we weren't concerned about anything but the cold. Although it was March, it was still winter. In fact, it had started snowing lightly.

Snow was one of the things I loved most about Alaska. I had a friend who hated the snow and every time it snowed, my phone would ring.

"I guess you're happy." Eunice would say. "You've been praying for snow again, haven't you?"

On this day snow was the last thing we needed. We were stuck between an avalanche and a collapsed bridge, with three small children and no way to communicate with the outside world. Our car radio could receive no signal since the mountains blocked the transmission.

As if reading my mind, my husband said, "You know the highway crews are really good in this area. They'll have that avalanche cleared soon. Let's go back and see if there's anyone at the camp."

Silvertip Camp was a small highway camp, providing housing and support buildings for the road crews in the area. These were the only buildings allowed in this part of the Chugach National Forest, so they became the gathering place for those of us stuck in the pass. Several other travelers had already arrived and stragglers continued to drift in over the next hour or so.

By the time we got to the camp the earthquake was an hour old and the camp manager was on his two-way radio. The reports trickling in described serious damage in many areas of South-central Alaska. My chest tightened when we heard that Seward had been wiped out, and Anchorage leveled. We later learned that these reports of damage were exaggerated, but it made for some gut-wrenching hours waiting for more accurate news.

By evening there were over twenty of us at the camp, including a young pregnant woman who was experiencing contractions. This was particularly worrisome when we discovered her last child was a cesarean delivery. As the news about Seward worsened she became hysterical. "I left my baby in Seward with my grandma and she lives down by the harbor. I have to get there now. I have to help them! My grandma is too old to do this by herself!"

Her husband tried to comfort her, but the young mother's panic increased as night fell. She turned to her husband "I'm leaving now. I'm going to walk and I don't care if you go with me or not. I've got to get to my baby."

We were sixty miles north of Seward. The camp manager got on the radio and arranged for another highway crew to meet the couple on the other side of the avalanche and transport them to Seward. All of us breathed a sigh of relief, both because we joined her in her concern for her child and because none of us felt competent to deliver a baby. We knew even if the Seward hospital was damaged there would at least be someone with medical experience to assist. I thanked God that our family was together and safe.

The camp manager's wife, accustomed to feeding the crews that came into camp, put a large moose roast on to cook. She began delegating chores, partly to get our minds off our fear, but also to get all the people fed. I had packed potato salad and fried chicken for our dinner since I knew we would get to the cabin too late to cook. Several others also had food, and as we put the finishing touches on dinner the manager's wife turned to me and commented, " Well, it seems like you did a pretty good job of packing for an earthquake."

Ours were the only children in the camp, so we fed them first and sent them out to play while the adults ate and discussed the situation. Just as we were finishing dinner the kids came running back in yelling, "There's a man out there."

The camp manager went to the door, "Chuck. What the hell are you doing on foot? Where's your car?"

"Well, I was at Alyeska shooting avalanches and got stuck on the other side of the bridge that's out. I was afraid you might be gone for the weekend. I sure am glad to see you."

"You mean you walked all the way here?"

"Didn't have a choice. Couldn't get my car across the bridge. I was able to pick my way across on foot and I figure I'm in good enough shape to walk on home."

"You're a darn fool. Why didn't you go on back to Anchorage?"

"Because my wife and kids are in Moose Pass. Besides I'm already about a third of the way there. Anyway, I figured I'd find someone who would give me a ride."

Chuck O'Leary, a Chugach forest ranger who specialized in avalanches, had been "shooting" the slopes with a cannon at Alyeska Ski Resort, a periodic chore performed to release the snow pressure in an attempt to avoid large avalanches. He and his team had just shot off a round when the earthquake occurred and the slopes dissolved into a mass of tumbling snow. At first they thought they had hit the wrong spot and triggered a massive slide.

His arrival was a welcome diversion. Finally, someone had some news. He reported that Alyeska was essentially still in one piece, although the Seward Highway had sunk several feet and was being covered by water at high tide. He had no new information about Anchorage.

Our family was given the use of the manager's mobile home. He and his wife assured us that there was no way they were going to sleep, so we might as well put the children in their bed rather than on the floor. I slept on the couch, or at least I tried to. We were having constant aftershocks and every time I put my head down, the world spun. Sharing the trailer with us was a large German Shepherd, who would sense an aftershock coming and begin whining and shaking. When he wasn't trying to claw his way under the couch, he was trying to crawl under my covers. The kids, on the other hand, slept like angels.

Bob stayed with the manager and the other adults listening to the radio in the office. He came to the trailer periodically and gave me the latest news. We heard that half of Anchorage had fallen into the Inlet and most of downtown had collapsed causing hundreds of deaths. The more news that came in, the more fearful we were for our friends.

The road crew set up lights and worked through the night to clear the avalanche, finishing the job by mid-morning. Among the stranded was a colonel from the Corps of Engineers and his wife. A military helicopter came in early that morning to pick them up and transport them back to Anchorage. The helicopter added to the carnival atmosphere for the children. They were wildly excited to see such a marvelous machine up close.

Since we couldn't get back to Anchorage because of the collapsed bridge, the cabin on Kenai Lake seemed the safest place to go, but we had only a quarter tank of gas and had been told by the helicopter pilot that the only vehicles allowed gas were "necessary" vehicles. Since Chuck was an avalanche expert and needed to be available he commandeered our car (with us in it) to take him to his home near Kenai Lake where he could be in contact with his office. Because he was a ranger, he could get us gas at Moose Pass.

Just past the avalanche, a long gracefully curving bridge crossed high above Canyon Creek. It was one of the few large bridges that remained standing after the earthquake, probably because it was built of steel rather than concrete. I was sure it would collapse, killing us all.

Everyone in camp attempted to reassure me, telling me that they had been running heavy machinery across it all night. "Yes," I said, "but now you've weakened it so much that the first car across will be the straw that breaks the camel's back".

We made it across the bridge without even the slightest tremor, although I held my breath the whole time. We stopped several times for Chuck to take pictures of the avalanches along the way. Although he was worried about his family, he was fascinated with how the snow on the mountains had reacted to the earthquake. He and Bob had a long conversation about the intricacies of different types of snow and slopes and what had happened. I couldn't believe they were discussing snow.

We stopped for gas at a small station where Chuck knew the owner. He got the news that his family was safe, but he was anxious to see for himself. When we pulled into the yard of his home, his children tumbled from the door of the house with his wife close behind.

She was wonderfully calm. "Well, I was wondering when you would show up!" She greeted him with a hug as the children clung to any piece of him that they could reach.

"Everything is fine here," she said. "You even missed most of the clean up. We didn't have much damage, but you probably need to check on some of the older folks around here to see if they need some help."

Chuck and his wife insisted on giving us moose and goat meat from their freezer, which we gladly took since we had no idea how long it would be before we could return home.

As we approached the cabin my emotions were in turmoil. "What if the cabin has collapsed? Where will we stay if it has?" I had led a reasonably easy life and I wasn't sure I was up to this challenge.

The cabin was still standing, although the refrigerator was turned on its side and everything in the cabinets had dumped out. Glass shards and dried food covered the floor, so I set about cleaning the place while Bob checked the foundation. The children, glad to be out of the car, played happily in the snow. Everything was peaceful if you didn't count the continuous aftershocks.

Bob was helping me set the refrigerator back upright when the kids burst through the front door yelling, "There's a big moose in the yard." We went to the window and sure enough there stood a large bull moose with a wild look in his eye. I wasn't the only one being driven to distraction by the aftershocks.

That evening we built a roaring fire and let the kids roast marshmallows and make s'mores. They were in heaven, especially when they were told they could sleep on mattresses in front of the fireplace that night. Their day had been full of adventure and excitement, so they dozed off easily. Bob and I sat in front of the fire, speaking softly about the earthquake that had shaken our lives a mere thirty hours earlier.

The next morning we were awakened by a loud thwacking sound outside the cabin. The children ran out to investigate. Bill burst back into the room. He said, "There's a helicopter outside and Mr. Coger is leaning out the door waving to us." Bob and I rushed outside in time to see one of Bob's co-workers from the gas company hanging out of the helicopter circling above us. He waved and yelled for us to meet them at the Sunrise Inn.

By the time we had all dressed and driven to the inn, Bill Coger and the pilot had almost finished their breakfast. We joined them for coffee and caught up on all the news. Coger assured us that all of our friends were safe, but that the city we had grown to love was severely damaged. Because of ruptured lines the city's gas supply had been shut down and was now being reconnected street by street. All the employees, even the executives, like Bob, were helping. They needed Bob to return to Anchorage. Bill Coger turned to me and said, "You know you and the kids will be safer here where you have electricity and heat. You wouldn't have that in Anchorage."

I must have looked skeptical about being left behind, because he added, "Besides, I told your folks that you were safe when they called the office and I don't want to have lied to them."

With reports of bears spotted in the vicinity of our cabin, we decided to move to the Sunrise Inn until Bob could return for us. We packed hurriedly, transferring the essentials into our small room in the motel. We would eat our main meals at the restaurant there, so we didn't bother packing food. As I watched the helicopter take off, tears filled my eyes, but I quickly brushed them away. I didn't want the children to see how upset I was that Bob was leaving.

Fortunately the inn had a large radio antenna that could pick up stations from Anchorage. With all of the phone lines down, our only source of communication was through an Anchorage radio program that broadcast personal messages. In this way we could receive dispatches, but couldn't send them. The next morning when the children and I arrived in the restaurant for breakfast we were told there had been a message from Bob. The winds would have to die down before they could get in with a small plane to pick us up. Winds were always squirrelly across Turnagain Arm, but especially in the spring, so this wasn't a big surprise, just another disappointment.

The next few days were a blur of tense sameness. The winds continued to blow, so the children and I had little to do but wait. We often drove to the shattered Kenai Bridge and looked longingly at the other side where life seemed to have returned to near normal. We would occasionally see the daring individual who leaped from ice floe to ice floe on the wide, turbulent river, risking his life to deliver our mail. One slip and he would have been crushed to death or drowned. His bravery made us feel less cut off from the rest of the world. In the days following the earthquake, the Post Office wasn't requiring postage on outgoing mail from Alaska, so I wrote my parents and other family members often.

The state of Alaska sent in a public health nurse to give everyone typhoid vaccinations to protect against the possibility that the drinking water had become tainted. It seemed a reasonable thing to do and the older children suffered only slight discomfort, complaining of sore arms and aches. Two-year-old Karen, on the other hand, had a severe reaction with high fever and chills. I held and rocked her all night, swabbing her with cool damp rags to reduce her sky-high fever. I'd never felt so alone or afraid.

On Friday, one week after the earthquake, we finally got the news that Bob would be in to pick us up in a small plane. Gas and electricity had been restored to our house and it was safe for us to return. The children were really excited at the prospect of seeing their father again, no more so than I. It had been a long week, and I was ready to get back to a normal life.

The plane arrived and the kids swarmed over their father. Bill grabbed his dad's hand and began telling him about all the wild animals he had seen. Valerie demanded to be picked up, and Karen attached herself to his leg like a koala bear on a tree. I hugged him close and told him how much I had missed him. It was good to be together again.

We attempted to settle my hotel bill, but the owners wouldn't accept payment, insisting that in a disaster they didn't expect to be rewarded. This was an attitude that we discovered over and over during the coming weeks. The stories of courage and generosity were a balm after our lives had been so badly shaken.

The pilot of the small plane that Bob had hired to pick us up was quite concerned about having three small children inside his newly refurbished interior. He had just installed new carpet and seats in the cabin, and had visions of children throwing up all over them

"Here, son, you're old enough to hold this bag in front of you in case you start feeling sick, and Mom, you hold the baby in your lap and put a bag under her chin."

That left Bob with Valerie and her barf bag. Although the flight across the Inlet was rough, our seasoned little Alaskans were much more interested in looking out the window than in throwing up. The pilot flew straight into Merrill Field, so we didn't get to see much of the damage from the air, but on the drive home we dodged deep cracks that crisscrossed the road. A few of the buildings slanted sideways on their foundations as if they had had one drink too many.

Home again. The house didn't look too damaged, although Bob had told me that one wall in the basement had collapsed, bowing inward, where a fissure had run through the yard and into the house. Most of our wedding china and crystal had broken.

"How about the pottery?"

"No, none of that."

"Rats!"

I hated the pink pottery that my mother had talked me into choosing when I was making my wedding selections, and was hoping I would have a good excuse to buy a new pattern. Not even one piece was broken! Years later I sold it at a garage sale to a missionary who took it to a village on the Bering Sea where, I'm sure, it all remains unchipped.

When I walked into the house I was amazed. I expected everything to be askew, but it was quite neat. Later I discovered that Bob had spent several evenings cleaning up the living room and kitchen so I wouldn't be so distressed when I first entered the house.

The bedrooms were another matter. Chests of drawers were overturned with all their contents on the floor. Clothes had been flung from the closet and were scattered around the room. The children's toys were in even more chaotic disarray than usual. It looked like the aftermath of a burglary.

"I'll clean this up later. I want to see the basement wall," I said to Bob.

The unfinished basement, with its gray walls, and concrete floor, looked about the same except for the odd bow in the front wall. It had cracked about three feet up from the floor and collapsed inward as if it had been hit with a huge sledgehammer.

I was walking toward the wall to get a better look when I heard a deep rumble and the floor began to move. Bob grabbed both our daughters and pushed Bill toward the stairs. "Get upstairs. Now!" he yelled.

"Oh no," I said, "not again!"

The aftershock we felt in the basement was the final straw for many people. I knew one man who handed his friend the keys to his eighth floor apartment, telling him, "I'm leaving the state. You're welcome to anything you have the courage to go up there and get."

Our parents begged us to return to Texas to live, but we loved Alaska. Our adopted home had gained the dubious distinction as the site of the largest earthquake to hit North America, but it also was populated with people who were filled with pioneer spirit. They were anxious to rebuild what had been lost, and we knew we wanted to be there, working beside them.

During the weeks following the earthquake we learned that only the nine deaths in Anchorage were attributed directly to the shaking of the quake, but another one hundred and six Alaskans lost their lives in the huge waves that followed. The low tide, the afternoon occurrence of the quake, and the fact that it was a holiday prevented the death toll from being higher.

But downtown Anchorage looked like a war zone with Fourth Avenue split down the middle and half of it sinking several feet while the other half buckled upward. Entire blocks of homes built on a bluff in the Turnagain Heights subdivision had slid into Cook Inlet after the earth under them liquefied during the quake. Damage was even worse in other parts of Alaska with Valdez and the village of Chenega being virtually wiped out by the tsunami, while Whittier was severely damaged when some glaciers broke off, falling into the sea, causing a huge wave to cover the waterfront. We realized how lucky we had been to be in a relatively undamaged area.

We never learned what happened to the young couple from Seward, only that a large section of Seward's waterfront slid into Resurrection Bay, creating a local tsunami causing massive damage. The town was hit again twenty minutes later by the open-water tsunami. We could only hope that their child and grandmother survived.

As we put our house back in order, we continued to hear stories of amazing courage and knew we had made the right decision to remain in Alaska. Even though the occasional aftershock made our hearts beat a little faster and there was always the possibility of another big earthquake, we knew this was home. Alaska had etched a place in our hearts even the Great Alaskan Earthquake couldn't shake loose. ❧

❧

Trees, mountains, and cars whizzed by. Kids bickered and the radio played. I do remember stopping in Washington. The doctor looked at me and then at my husband. "We only have about two thousand miles to go," Jim said.

Kathy Hughes

There's No Place Like Home

Surviving a 5000-mile trip with four children and pneumonia

by Kathy Hughes

Kathy Hughes lives in Anchorage with her husband Jim, their four children, and granddaughter. She was born in the Alaskan Territory and experienced Statehood and the Great Alaska Earthquake. Her husband's military career led them throughout the world, but after retirement they found their way back home to Alaska. She is working on a creative writing degree by correspondence from Brigham Young University, and writing an Alaskan children's novel. ✍

"YOU HAVE PNEUMONIA," the doctor told me.

"Am I going to die?"

He looked at me over the top of his glasses. "No."

My eyes closed. No such luck.

"I want to see you again in three days," he added.

"I won't be here. In three days I'll be about a thousand miles up the road." We had already driven fifteen hundred miles and what started out as a slight cold had blossomed through the high Colorado Mountains.

The United States Army was transferring my husband Jim from Fort Sam Houston, Texas to Fort Richardson, Alaska. The plan included driving and sailing every inch of the way during the month of February with four kids under the age of eight in a mid-sized Ford Fairmont. The plan didn't include pneumonia.

Changing duty stations wasn't new to us. Jim was "Career Army." Wherever we went, we went together and home was where the Army sent us. We took the good along with the bad. Touring the Alamo, exploring Mammoth Cave and viewing Mount Rushmore ranked high. Cockroaches dropping from the ceiling into my dinner plate, and snakes popping out of the dirt into my face made me wish I could tap my heels together, utter the words, "There's no place like home," and be magically transported. And now it was happening.

My father followed his dreams and moved his young family to the last frontier of Alaska in 1945. I was born there. I knew long winters filled with sledding, skating and walks to and from school in freezing weather. Summertime was filled with unending light. A softball game regularly started up about 8:00 p.m. and I played with my brothers until our mother called us in. The hard part was going to bed while the sun was still shining.

The doctor let me go with a promise I would stop at Madigan Hospital at Fort Lewis, Washington. With a prescription in my hand, I started to leave. The doctor called out, "You do realize you won't be able to nurse your baby while you're on this medication."

Oh great, now I'd have a mad, hungry baby to add to the plan, and what about all my milk?

We piled back into the car with Jim and two kids in the front seat and two in the back with me. We had nine hundred miles to go before I checked in with the next doctor, followed by a two and a half day ferry trip up the coast of Alaska. That left only an additional eight hundred miles to drive before we could bed down in temporary quarters at Fort Richardson. It would have been too much, except I was going home.

Unaccustomed to strong medicine, I lost my grip on reality. Were the kids talking or was slush hitting the windshield? It all sounded the same. It was time to feed the baby. My body knew it and so did he. The milk let loose. "Help," I managed to say as my head lolled sideways.

"Was that your mother?" Jim asked seven-year-old Jonathan sitting next to him. Just then the baby whacked me across the chest with his outstretched arm. Pain seared through me. I was dying. I could see it now, the epitaph on my tombstone, beloved mother struck down.

We rounded a curve somewhere in Idaho and my head rolled towards the window. A sharp cliff dropped away. It would be so easy, I thought, just open the door. No, I had too much to live for. "There's no place like Nome," I slurred, "there's no place like Nome."

"Was that your mother?"

"I think so, she's saying something about the phone," six-year-old Jennifer said.

Hours dragged by, slowly forming days. Sometimes the car stopped and my family rolled me out, fed me, and put me to bed. I coughed and choked through the long night and then morning came and the whole ordeal started again.

Trees, mountains, and cars whizzed by. Kids bickered and the radio played. I do remember stopping in Washington. The doctor looked at me and then at my husband. "We only have about two thousand miles to go," Jim said.

The doctor sighed. "Have them check her as soon as you get there." Jim walked me out to the car and buckled me in.

That evening we boarded the ferry. Our cabin was in the bow of the ship. We were the first to cut through icy waves. We would be the first to hit rocks or glaciers. We could all be wiped out in a matter of minutes. I lay on my bunk rolling from side to side. The burning pain in my swollen chest competed with the nausea rising from my stomach. The few times I was able to get up I knocked into walls as the ferry rocked.

For two days and nights we sailed north. Finally we reached the port of Haines, Alaska. Inhaling frigid air startled my lungs and I launched into a violent coughing spell. I grabbed my chest and the milk ducts opened. I felt my shirt grow wet and then cold.

While on the ferry my husband spoke with two other families being stationed in Anchorage. They agreed to form a convoy. It was a matter of good sense, the men agreed. The women nodded their heads in approval. We were glad for the company.

Once again we started off. I was feeling better and when we spotted nearly three hundred bald eagles in the trees my mind only briefly skipped to Alfred Hitchcock's "The Birds." They lined the road like sentinels guarding the way into the magic land of home. It was hard for Jim to keep his eyes on the icy highway, and the car skidded. I crashed back to reality as the shoulder belt bit into my chest.

We were last in line and we soon lost sight of our companions. In time we found one at rest in a ditch with a shattered window. Jim checked on them but the man reassured him, "We'll be fine, I called for a wrecker on my CB radio. He'll be here soon. You go ahead." We pulled back onto the road and I caught the desperate look in the woman's face as the last bit of civilization rolled away.

"Macho men," I said.

"Was that your mother?" Jim asked four-year old Jodi. Jodi rocked her head back and forth repeating something about big birdies coming to get her.

The highway left United States soil for Canadian and plenty of border crossing information lined the roadside. As we approached, my husband spotted the third car. "I wonder if they know about the car in the ditch." I mumbled. Busy pumping the brakes to slow down, he didn't answer.

I guess we'll never know what the other driver was thinking because without warning he sped through the border gate.

Sirens, lights, and warnings to stop blared out. They didn't even slow him down.

We pulled up and Jim yanked on the frozen window handle. "Hello folks," the officer said. "Sorry about all the fuss."

"What's going to happen to those people?" Jim asked.

"Oh, I've radioed ahead. They'll be stopped at the other gate. Welcome to Canada, drive safely." So much for the convoy, I thought.

Our destination was Tok, Alaska, with an overnight temperature of minus fifty degrees. "Our car isn't going to start in the morning in this temperature," Jim said that night as we rolled in. "I'm going to have to start it a few times."

"Go for it," I said as I fell onto the motel bed. I remembered hearing him get up and then how cold he was when he crawled back into bed next to me. I whacked him on the chest and told him to move over.

The second time he circled the one block downtown he commented that something seemed different. The next morning we learned the only grocery store in town had burned down. The firemen came, but at minus fifty degrees there wasn't a lot they could do.

Our last day in the car, we headed out on the final stretch with only three hundred and fifty miles to go. "I think I'm going to make it," I told Jodi.

"What's you gonna make, Mommy?" I smiled. I was going to make a new beginning. I had survived ten days in a mid-size car with four kids and my husband. I had survived pneumonia, the engorgement of a nursing mother, five thousand miles of highway, ice storms, flying slush, choppy waters, hovering birds, burning buildings and Canadian border runners. My family and I were home.

For the first year we lived in military quarters and then purchased our first house. Home now included our four kids, my husband, Grandma and Grandpa and our first house all in my hometown. I knew it couldn't get any better.

As time passed and one beautiful Alaskan season followed another I knew it wouldn't last. After four years, my husband began talking about our next assignment and I thought about leaving. How could I? This was home. No, home is where the Army sends you. No, this was home.

It wasn't an option to leave the Army. We had already invested fourteen years and Jim was determined to see it through to retirement. We would have to leave.

When the time came we packed up, rented the house, kissed the relatives goodbye and headed out in our motor home. We hit the Alcan Highway and for the next six years we lived in northern Virginia, southern Alabama and central Europe.

The comforts of my home in Alaska were a sharp, clear memory each time I met with difficulty. When temperatures soared into one hundred degrees plus, and jelly fish stung me, I remembered home. As I huddled on the kitchen floor hoping the tornado would miss our quarters, I thought of home. And finally when it was over I flew with four kids from Frankfurt, Germany to Los Angeles to Seattle and then the last leg of our journey to Anchorage. I was back and I was happy.

There's no place like home. ✧

❦

As I started my fourth day, and shredded my finger on yet another paper edge, I considered my work schedule. I would be filing seven days a week, twelve-plus hours a day, with thirty minutes for lunch. Further, I would commute from another camp on a bus traveling forty minutes each way. I would have to face down four hundred and fifty guys to get my meals.

Janet McCart

Pipeliner

*One woman among a thousand men
on the TransAlaska Pipeline*

by Janet McCart

Janet McCart came to Alaska in the high days
of the pipeline, and polyester leisure suits. She's
never again worn a powder-blue pants suit.
Janet resides in Anchorage, Alaska, with her
husband Dick and her co-dependent Friends of
Pets dog Tessa. Her novels include *Forgiving Rose*
and *Failing Upward.*

THE THIRTY-FIVE PIPEFITTERS were wearing ballcaps that looked like they'd been made from June Cleaver's old dresses. The fact that they were pipefitters was apparently supposed to offset the floral cotton prints. I was the only woman in the classroom, and I wasn't wearing a cap. I felt as if I'd crossed into the Twilight Zone.

"We are retired Marine drill sergeants!" one of the instructors announced with arms crossed and booted feet firmly set. "We have the power to send you home with your tail between your legs!"

"Today, over the next six hours," the other Marine drill sergeant shouted, "you will learn about environmental safety, personal safety, Arctic safety, health—" he paused and glanced at me "—and sexually transmitted diseases."

A blush rose up my neck.

We sat through a slide show featuring what frost-bite and sexually transmitted disease could do to human tissue. We heard about the dangers of metals fracturing, and oil becoming solid at forty below zero. We heard about the danger of drinking vodka that had sat out all night in those same temperatures. (Imagine if you will, frostbite of the mouth, esophagus, and stomach.) We saw instructional tapes about how to deal with black bears, polar bears, and moose. We were warned that many arctic fox carry rabies. We were instructed to take baths daily.

Some took exception. There were threats to walk out. But for me there was no turning back.

This job was my Mom's idea; she was thrilled that my Uncle Pat could get me a job on the pipeline. The fact that the TransAlaska Pipeline is eight hundred miles long and routed through some of the most forbidding terrain on earth did not dampen her spirits.

I'd had five days to quit my job, move out of my rental house, pack, and fly to another world — Alaska. Friends and family kicked in to help.

"You should look nice for your new job," my mother said. "We need to go get you some nice, new clothes."

"Mom, I'm going to work on the pipeline. I don't think they dress up for that."

"You always need to look your best, even on the pipeline." So, we went shopping and she bought me stylish suede boots, a powder-blue jacket and pantsuit, and two pairs of wool slacks with matching blouses and scarves. Everything was packed into a huge, hot-pink Samsonite suitcase that shone like neon among the olive green duffel bags piled at the back of the classroom. After classes and a ream of paper work we were loaded onto buses and sent careening through town to various medical offices for our physicals. As I stood in a little cubicle changing into a paper robe so I could join in a line-style physical with thirteen men, panic set in. I wasn't giving up my underwear!

To all our relief, a nurse pulled me out of the fidgeting group of men. After the physical, hearing test, vision test, spinal exam, and blood work, we were loaded back into vans for the trip to Anchorage International Airport.

Another drill sergeant announced: "You will be going to one of four destinations: Prudhoe Bay, Cold Foot, Pump Station Eight, or Valdez." My name was called as part of the Valdez contingent. Nine of us were packed onto a ten-seat plane. "Where's the rest room?" I asked a pilot who looked as if he had yet to graduate from high school.

He pointed to a tin coffee can on the floor. The can looked rusted. I wasn't sure if he was kidding or not.

The flight started out rough and got worse. I started praying. At one point, the teen pilots took out a map. One series of bounces threw all our carry-ons to the back of the plane. Finally, we were slam-dunked on to a strip of tarmac ringed by jagged mountains, and delivered to the modern airplane terminal. There was mud everywhere.

A driver found us, and told us ours was the only plane to make it in during the whole day. Weren't we the lucky ones? He took us to his mud-covered van. The world was gray and the rain was relentless. Forty minutes later we pulled up to the Induction Center. I stepped from the van into ankle deep mud — so much for the suede boots.

Inside, a large, block-shaped woman with deep frown lines shouted, "Stand in line at the arrows on the floor and listen up! No drugs, no booze, no ladies of the evening in your rooms!

We recommend you take a shower at least every other day!
Meals are served morning and night at both of the two-thou-
sand-man mess halls! You take your lunch with you from the
mess hall! Security will check your badges everywhere you
go! Craft people must get brass and check through the brass
shacks coming and going from the job!"

As I was contemplating what brass was, and why the
crafts-people needed to check it, she frowned at me and pointed.
"You, get last in line."

She took badge pictures and stamped out strange little brass
discs, and gave out room keys to the eight guys in front of me
and sent them on their way. There wasn't much conversation
going on.

Then she came to me.

"What's brass?" I asked.

She eyed me, identifying me as a cheechako. "It's a number identifying the hourly craft guys. Brass is used to clock in
and clock out."

She flipped open huge barracks' room charts. "There's only
one woman's barracks. I don't have room for another woman
in this camp. You'll have to go back over to Keystone Camp,
girly."

With that, she did my paperwork, and shoved me in front
of a colored sheet to take my photo. The pasty-white girl on
my badge was a picture that would haunt me for a long time
to come.

"Okay, girly," she said, "Next you go across the road and
get your hard hat at that shack over there." She pointed
through a muddy window.

"I don't think I'll need one of those."

"Honey," she snapped, "you're on a construction site now.
Wake up and smell the coffee. Get your damn hard hat or go
home."

Crossing the road sounds so simple, but a seemingly infi-
nite number of buses full of workers rolling out the gates allowed no foot traffic. Finally, one stopped to let me wade
across and I got my last piece of gear—the hard hat with my
name on it. It sat high on my wet head like a chicken looking
for a place to roost. I slung my purse on one shoulder, my

shoulder bag on the other, and grabbed my hot-pink suitcase and marched outside.

One of the ubiquitous Carharrt-clad men pulled up in a truck to yell, "Why are you standing in the rain like you don't have sense?"

"I'm supposed to go to Keystone Camp, and I don't know how."

"I'm not supposed to do this with the union agreements and all," he said as he loaded my stuff in his truck, "but I don't know how you are supposed to get there either."

The Camp Coordinator, a tall woman in tight western jeans, surveyed me and my pink suitcase. She flashed me a quick don't-latch-on-to-me smile, and welcomed me to the camp. She handed me keys for my room and mailbox and a gray wool blanket. "You go over two buildings, down four, and across three and make a left." I nodded, grabbed my load, and went out the door. A sea of yellow and white tin buildings stood in front of me. I walked a few feet and plopped everything in the mud. My mind went blank. Finally, I saw another woman and followed her where ever she was going.

The barracks were aluminum-sided, modular ATCO trailers, set to form a single-story block of rooms surrounding the laundry, shower, and toilet facilities. They smelled like industrial cleaner and wet wool. The halls were floored with gray, worn linoleum. The rooms had orange paisley indoor-outdoor carpets. Each room held twin beds separated by a small, battered desk. In the tiny space at the end of each bed was a microscopic closet. Gold vinyl curtains hung in the small windows. My bedroom walls were lined with dark paneling that was so thin I could hear breathing in the next room. The beds were made up with white sheets and one gray wool blanket each. I had been privileged to get an extra one.

I wandered to the center of the structure. The laundry room, and the bathroom were in use, but it looked to me as if there were only a handful of women in the whole place. Shower curtains didn't cover the showers and a row of rust-stained sinks.

On top of that, I had no idea where to get food, how to get back over to the main camp of five thousand people in the morning, or where to go once I got there. A woman wearing dirty overalls, knee-high rubber boots, and a hard-hat stomped into the barracks and stopped at the sight of me, and my pink luggage.

She paused at my door. "What's the matter kid?"

I took a deep breath and told her all the things I didn't know.

She listened, sized me up, and said, "It's Valdez, with a hard *e*." She shook her head. "Okay, listen up. The mess hall is just two blocks in front of us, but it's about to close. The Rec Hall is about three rows back, and you get your mail and some snacks there." She paused. "I don't think you're with craft. What do you do?"

"Office type stuff, typing, filing, transcription..."

She nodded. "There are two categories of workers on the construction site: staff and craft. Staff jobs are stuff like management, admin, personnel, quality control, engineering, and office gals — pretty much non-union. Craft jobs are the pipefitters, electricians, laborers, Teamsters, iron workers — mostly union.

"You need to catch the staff bus at five-thirty in the morning. It's marked on the end of the second row. That should get you to the right places. You okay now?"

I nodded, nearly bowing at her feet.

She strolled down the hall to her room. I swear, from somewhere I heard the song: "Welcome to the Hotel California. You can check out, but you can never leave."

I couldn't face the mess hall that night and pulled a few crumpled packs of crackers from my purse. I didn't sleep much, anxious about nearly everything I could think of, including getting up on time and group-showering. I needn't have worried. If the umpteen diesel buses gunning and idling nearby, and the women banging through the tin showers, and the cassette players blasting hadn't awakened me, I would have been in a coma. But, somehow, I didn't think a little coma would be considered a good excuse for missing work here.

In the morning the women seemed to be on auto-pilot as they showered, brushed their teeth, blew dry, and used the rest rooms. This provided its own sort of privacy. I donned my cute powder-blue pantsuit with matching scarf, my soft blue jacket, and because I had no others, I put my suede boots back on. I marched, helmet in hand, to the mess hall.

Outside rain poured down as I wound my way through a maze of buses. The combined smell of mess-hall bacon, diesel, and wet wool is imprinted on my brain from those mornings. Finally, I found the bus marked "staff" and climbed on board to sit in the first seat behind the bus driver's.

I was tapped firmly on the shoulder by a bearded, Carharrts-clad man. "That's Tiny's seat," he said. He was serious. "Since you're a 'girl,' and since he's sick, you can sit there today."

"Are you sure?" I asked.

He wasn't.

"You can have this seat back here as yours," a slight man with a beard hollered.

I made my way back and sat next to him on the aisle. "It takes seniority to get window seats," he explained. "They're the best for leaning against to sleep."

I nodded, worried I was going to make a fool of myself in front of fifty very serious men. Everyone on the bus was intent on helping me find my place of work. I got a lot of sympathy and guidance. So I confided to the fellow next to me about the mean woman at the induction center. "She made me go get this helmet," I declared.

"HELMET!" he howled, grabbing it out of my reach. "Did you hear that everybody? She called this a HELMET! I guess we must be in a war zone." Ha-ha-ha.

"Kick me in the leg," he said.

"No, that's okay." I smiled, wondering if he was crazy.

"Come on, kick me." He poked and teased until I finally kicked him. His leg was aluminum.

The staffers on the bus, mostly QC (quality control) guys, bid me farewell at one of dozens of ATCO aluminum buildings. It turned out to be the right one. The administration building was configured in eight double-trailers end-on-end — this was one banana of a building. I finally found my way to my new boss.

The administration manager was from Texas. His skin was the color of yellow wax, and he looked like he deeply regretted signing on for this one last job before retirement.

"Great, another *&^%$#*! political hire," he said to the ceiling. "What am I supposed to do with her? I don't need another dead weight. Why didn't anyone *#*!*(^ tell me she was coming?"

Then to me he said, "Please tell me that you at least have a few #@*#!@& office skills. The last political hire was so bad I sat her down with a typewriter and a ream of paper and told her to type something and throw it in the trash."

I said that I did in fact have some office skills. He grunted and shoved himself out of his chair. "What have you got that hard-hat stuck on your silly head for? Do you think the roof's gonna cave in? You'll be lucky to make it a week." He went down the hall yelling.

His secretary came to my rescue. "Don't worry about him, he's always gruff. My name is Ross. You look awful. For heaven's sake, get rid of this thing!" She pinched my tuna and onion sandwich from the bag and removed it from the room. She came back to her desk, sat down, and stared at me. "Your face is green."

"I'm okay," I mumbled, "just point me to the bathroom."

When I came back, she had hot tea with a little sugar, and a pile of soda crackers waiting for me. I'd met my first pipeline friend.

I was delivered to a conference room stacked with at least sixty boxes and uncounted bags of unorganized records. They were piled to the ceiling, and shoved under and on top of the huge conference table. "File these by the Dewey Decimal System," ordered a pock-faced man dressed entirely in black.

I had no idea what that meant. "Sure," I said. I pushed through stacks of paper, and opened boxes in a quest for Dewey and his Decimal System. Luckily, all the papers had little numbers in the right corner, so I started putting them in order, which was accidentally right.

People stopped by to introduce themselves. Each one said, "Pace yourself." I'd never heard of a job where one was advised to "pace." Was this a little initiation trick? I plowed into the sea of papers like the low-life, unwanted, political hire I was. I'd never seen a clock move more slowly.

As I started my fourth day, and shredded my finger on yet another paper edge, I considered my work schedule. I would be filing seven days a week, twelve-plus hours a day, with thirty minutes for lunch. Further, I would commute from another camp on a bus traveling forty minutes each way. I would have to face down four hundred and fifty guys to get my meals. I would have to inhale diesel fumes morning and night. My roommate, a hot-tempered redhead, sat up at two every morning to smoke an unfiltered Pall Mall. She went back to sleep while I considered putting a pillow firmly over her head.

There was no way I could yell uncle because my uncle had stuck his neck out to get me this job. With overtime I was making four times my old salary. So, I hunkered down. Day after day I told myself, just one more day.

Fortunately, after six long days, a woman in personnel got mad and drug up. (Dragging up was pipeline lingo for quitting, versus a case of the red-ass, which describes exactly how the person felt just before he or she quit.) With the other woman's departure, I had a job doing personnel work.

Getting through the first weeks was an endurance test. I learned the value of pacing. I later found out that six out of seven people drug up before spending two weeks on the site.

When Ross figured I was going to hang in there, she took me to Valdez proper, and to the bank. Friday evening at the bank was a social event. Every teller window was open. Carhartt-clad workers lined up out the door as tellers loudly counted out the amount each person took in cash. "Two thousand one hundred, three thousand one hundred!" We listened to their totals, figuring who had the biggest check of the week. It was always a pipefitter/calibrator. Our checks, as clerical workers, were about one quarter of those of the crafts.

Shops in Valdez were stocked like the old general stores — there was a little bit of everything you could imagine. It wasn't cheap, but it was available. I bought rubber boots, jeans, warm shirts, a rain jacket, and the appropriate duffel bag. I learned to call my stuff gear, instead of clothes or luggage. I mail-ordered a down parka and snow boots for winter. My cute outfits were mailed home. In turn, my family sent me my afghan and an electric popcorn popper.

Every Saturday night, the gals and I hopped the bus to town. We stopped at the Pipeliner Club for Hawaiian pupus, and then headed to one of the three dance joints. Club owners imported fabulous Las Vegas bands that played until four in the morning. No female ever paid for a drink or sat out a song. Regardless of how late we headed home we were up and at our desks by six-thirty!

As construction neared completion, the pink RIF (reduction in force) slips flew. Finally, it was my turn. I took the last pipeline commuter bus from Valdez to Anchorage, as the construction crew turned the terminal over to the production crew.

Who would have thought an adventure that started with so many challenges would deliver one of the great adventures of my life? If I could handle the hours and conditions of work on the pipeline, I could handle anything.

And now I know always to wear a hard hat but never to wear a powder-blue pantsuit to a construction site. ৵

᪥

We stood motionless, six people who had lost their minds, three thousand feet above base camp at the top of a glacier with no way down but to ski. And we had actually paid money to do this.

Betty Monthei

Playing in God's Backyard

Taking on Thompson's Pass with airplane and ski

by Betty Monthei

Betty moved from Oregon to Alaska with her husband Lee in 1980 in search of adventure. They planned a two-year stay and haven't left yet, except for a one-year hiatus in The Federated States of Micronesia. She has worked in a variety of secretarial and office positions and is now working full time as a writer. She has had two romances published (as Betty Jane Sanders) by Silhouette Books and has several projects in various stages of completion. As for finding adventure, she couldn't help but succeed in that endeavor being married to Lee. ✺

I HAVE OFTEN THOUGHT that you could find God on the drive between Valdez and Anchorage. Thompson Pass is one of the reasons. Rugged rock and snowy peaks studded with glaciers silently guard a land they have belonged to forever. Wilderness extends mile upon mile as far as the eye can see.

I was not in any hurry to find God that day, particularly since I figured it would be as a result of my death on a flight skiing trip out of Valdez.

Why did I go? I haven't a clue.

My husband, Lee, and I came to Alaska seeking adventure in 1980, planning a two-year stay. We finally settled in Anchorage. We worked the first year in Prudhoe Bay then returned to a more normal life. Lee added a Master of Science degree in Engineering Management from University of Alaska, Anchorage, and I started a career as an Escrow Officer. When Lee's employer asked him to move to Valdez in 1992, we jumped at the opportunity.

The eight hundred-mile TransAlaska Pipeline ends at Valdez, where mountains meet the sea. Tankers ride long and high into Valdez Arm and then leave a few hours later weighted down with Prudhoe Bay crude. Bewhiskered otters and seals cruise in and out of the small boat harbor. Black bear share your back yard. Eagles nest at the edge of subdivisions and in the fall perch along tree-lined rivers and creeks, stomachs filled with salmon.

We had been warned about the average snowfall of three hundred and fifty inches a year. Not a problem. Being avid skiers, we love snow. And snow we got. The problem was that the nearest ski slope was Alyeska Ski Resort, a twisting three hundred and forty-mile drive subject to whiteout and icy conditions. Air travel was expensive and often undependable due to weather.

So Lee decided we should try the plane skiing offered further up the Pass. This I did not want to do. Besides suffering terrible motion sickness in small planes, I loved life. I knew with absolute certainty that if I did not fall several hundred feet into a crevasse to lie there for days, cold and broken, suffering a lingering death, then an avalanche would bury me.

But one Saturday morning found us packing our ski gear and driving up the Pass. Clouds rose and fell and danced with the sun. Base camp was a parking lot, an ATCO trailer, and the familiar green porta-potty we Alaskans love to hate. A red and white Beaver plane waited, dwarfed by the surrounding mountains. It looked like a toy. Anyone with an ounce of sense would have backed out right then.

The folks in the base camp trailer suggested we carry avalanche locator beacons so that they could find our bodies in case something happened. Lee and I rented one each and strapped them beneath our ski jackets next to our hearts.

There were six of us; a father and teenaged son, Lee's boss and friend, Cliff, a friend of Cliff's, Lee and I. We waited in the parking lot, anxiously watching the sky. Clouds thickened and dropped. My heart lifted while the others wore long faces.

Cliff demonstrated his new ski poles that could be telescoped and turned into avalanche probes. He carried a backpack (not much larger than a daypack) filled with survival gear. I do not know what it contained. Probably a few granola bars, a folding shovel to dig out the bodies he would find with the ski poles, maybe a blanket, a small emergency tent, and some candles and matches. Not much considering there were six of us and he was the only one with a pack. I did not ask what happened if he were the one to fall into the glacier.

The clouds suddenly lifted. The pilot fired up the engine, gear was handed in, and we squashed into the narrow body of the plane.

The noise was deafening as we lurched into the air, then bounced and bucked our way above the mountains. My mouth filled with bitter metallic fear, and I swallowed hard against a wave of nausea. Not only was I going to die, I was going to disgrace myself by throwing up en route.

Finally the plane swooped toward a flat expanse of snow, skimmed the surface to test landing conditions, then shot past peaks and glaciers and fell into empty space. The contents of my stomach lurched upward. I bit my lip, prayed for mercy and for my breakfast to stay where it belonged. A quick death was beginning to sound good. As the plane shuddered I pushed away the image of all the screws and bolts popping loose. We sharply banked then climbed up and around again and landed with a roar.

"Stay to the right of the glacier to avoid the deep crevasses," the pilot shouted over the noise of the engine. We spilled from the plane, dragging skis and poles. I nearly fell to my knees and kissed the snow. Then the plane lumbered off, snow spraying beneath its skis before it lifted and disappeared around a peak.

Utter silence. We stood motionless, six people who had lost their minds, three thousand feet above base camp at the top of a glacier with no way down but to ski. And we had actually paid money to do this.

The air was beyond crisp, chilling my lungs with each breath and smelling only of cold. Dark snow-scattered peaks shot skyward to the right, to the left, everywhere I looked. Uneven patches of blue peeked through gray clouds which did little to diminish the brilliance of the snow. Untouched snow dotted with glacial blue stretched endlessly. The ridges and valleys below were in miniature.

We were mere specks of blues and reds in a world that could easily crush us with an avalanche, or watch us disappear over the lip of a crevasse. Cold hard silence pressed against us.

My heart expanded with unexpected joy. If I had to die, what a way to go!

We moved as one, stomping into skis and gripping poles, our chatter, laughter, and excitement swallowed by the silence surrounding us. Ours cheeks were red, noses numb. Clouds threatened once again to drop. It would be a very long night if the plane could not get in to pick us up in the valley below.

And then we were off, along the edge of the glacier and to the right. I cut through rubble and flew through knee-deep champagne powder, cold biting my cheeks and watering my eyes. Lee carved turns to my right and slightly ahead, snow spraying behind in a glistening arc, his red ski jacket a beacon. Shards of sunlight pierced the moving clouds and chased us on our way. We were a loosely knit unit of six hugging the slope, moving in unsynchronized motion down the mountain in a run that was exhilarating, heart stopping, as near perfect as possible.

The plane waited in the valley. We scrambled in, anxious to beat the ever-threatening clouds. Back at base we watched the weather once more. But the clouds darkened, thickened, and finally dropped too low for the plane to fly.

Although I was disappointed and even admitted as much to Lee (his grin said "I told you so" but he wisely refrained from actually speaking the words), I had a memory so perfect than even a repeat could not have matched it.

A memory of when we played in God's backyard. ⊷

❧

My Alaska is an urban Alaska.
In Anchorage, where I've worked
as a journalist since 1985, big-marts,
gas-n-go's and high rises share
the landscape with alpenglow,
brazen ravens and the occasional
ripple of northern lights, visible
from my driveway as I take out the
trash on bitter January nights.

Rosanne Pagano

Alaskan Woman

*One Connecticut woman's adaptation
to Alaskan life*

by Rosanne Pagano

An Anchorage-based writer and editor since 1985,
Rosanne Pagano has an easier time explaining why
she stays in Alaska than why she came in the first
place. Pagano has written for newspapers in
California, Utah, New Mexico and Alaska and
has contributed feature stories to *Alaska* magazine
and *We Alaskans*, the Sunday magazine of the
Anchorage Daily News. She is editor of two *Alaska
Geographic* books published in 1999 and is a former
Anchorage newswriter for The Associated Press. In
1989 Pagano reported from Valdez on the *Exxon
Valdez* oil spill for Alaska Public Radio and National
Public Radio. In 1999 she joined the University of
Alaska-Anchorage as a professor in the Journalism
and Public Communications department. She is
originally from Connecticut. ⌁

I CAME TO ALASKA A BRIDE in tears.

Today, after 17 years on the Last Frontier, I know I wasn't the first, or the last. "Why?" I found myself whispering over and over again those first years. "Why are wild animals, capable of kicking a person to death, permitted to roam the city? Why does gasoline cost so much when the pipeline that feeds the rest of the country is within driving distance of my front door? Why are the wages so inflated, the people so free-spending, the lawns so full of boats, campers, old cars and scrap lumber?" Why, why, why?

Like northern people everywhere, true Alaska women have learned to make do or do without, to adapt or quit complaining. Some of us learn faster than others.

My Alaska is an urban Alaska. In Anchorage, where I've worked as a journalist since 1985, big-marts, gas-n-go's and high rises share the landscape with alpenglow, brazen ravens and the occasional ripple of northern lights, visible from my driveway as I take out the trash on bitter January nights. To be an urban Alaska woman is to be adrift in contradictions until one learns to travel in and out of cultures. I have learned to be lipsticked and wear unsensible shoes if staying in town for a concert at Anchorage's performing arts center, and to go showerless for a few days while hauling plywood to our homestead cabin, two hundred miles north of Anchorage.

Snapshots of that sunny morning we departed from the tree-lined, beautifully zoned Boulder neighborhood of a graduate-school friend show a trim smiling blond man (my husband), a bearded man and his laughing wife (our hosts) and me, fresh from a bout of crying in my friend's upstairs bedroom. We are posed beside the Toyota packed with all my groom and I possessed: a couple of bicycles, my sewing machine, our bed, an assortment of kitchen goods and our dog, Bessie, rescued from the Albuquerque pound. Today I would leave nearly all of it on the curb and set off with the dog, the husband and the truck, not necessarily in that order. Alaska women know to keep only what endures and to hell with the rest.

Alaska was never my dream destination (that was Paris). I had no pinings for a yard full of sled dogs, a garden stuffed with five-foot cabbages or even a little log cabin to call my own. My brother and I are only the second generation to be born in the New World, our grandparents having immigrated from Sicily and northern Italy in the early 1900s. My parents, both raised speaking only Italian until they went to grade school, were dreaming big for their day when they built a three-bedroom ranch house in a New Haven suburb, just twenty minutes by turnpike from their own parents and siblings.

As a child I did not favor winter over summer, an early indication that I might not be suited to the subarctic. I spent my happiest hours on the Connecticut shore, bodysurfing the summer away as only a flat-chested twelve-year-old can. After college graduation, I immediately moved to Long Island where I took a writing job and lived alone in the downstairs flat of a large house with a view of Long Island Sound.

On the eve of my big move to Long Island, an aunt who'd come to visit turned to my mother and confided in a low voice I was not meant to hear that she was relieved when her own daughters, cousins my age, had not chosen college. "It changes them," the aunt said. My mother kept her gaze straight ahead, a cup of coffee and uneaten biscotti before her, and said nothing.

Historians tell us of the "good-time" girls who mined the men who mined the Klondike gold fields. Their mothers could not have been happy, either. My first neighbor in Anchorage, a retired teacher who moved from Ohio as a bride in the 1930s, once told me that her mother wished her daughter in the grave rather than in Alaska. "She said at least she could visit me there," my elderly friend recalled.

I have never asked my mother why she did not fret aloud when I announced plans to marry a man whom she and my father had met only once, a man who did dream of Alaska. Perhaps they didn't question our adventure because we pitched it as just that—a short lark by a couple of crazy honeymooners eager to soak up the midnight sun. "It's just for a year or so," we said. We meant it. Maybe those good-time girls who stayed decades to form the economic backbone of early Anchorage and Fairbanks plied the same line. Maybe they meant it, too.

Our first house, purchased two years after we arrived in Anchorage, was an eight hundred-square-foot log cabin two blocks from the downtown intersection where a neighbor kept Star the reindeer in a wire cage to delight passers-by. Our neighborhood was full of such only-in-Alaska scenes—to the north is a block-wide park that stretches for a mile that had once been used for an airplane landing strip. But local lore did not draw me to the little log house, among Anchorage's oldest. I craved a city, even if it was only downtown Anchorage. In 1987, when the state's economy was limper than a sunburned forget-me-not, Anchorage's downtown was a real estate footnote, disdained by the fashionable, who preferred the views from high above Potter Marsh, and overlooked by everyone else except occasional bargain hunters like us. We bought low and spent high to fix up the place, abiding for a short time with voles in the pantry and nothing but floor joists in the bathroom.

On closing day, I called my parents: "We bought a house!" My mother asked only "Where?" clearly hoping the answer would be somewhere other than Anchorage.

Our child would be born in Alaska, not New Mexico where I had fallen in love, not California where I went to university, not in Connecticut where my cousins now prospered in the suburbs. I was an Alaskan now, whatever that meant, and so would be our half-Italian, half-Southern child. My child would feel as alien in my hometown as I felt in his.

Daniel arrived in February. He looked like nobody either of us knew, a true omen, as it turns out, since at age 11, my son has been his own man for years, one of those crank frontier libertarians with a natural suspicion of authority. A pleasant, "Daniel, time for school!" might elicit an equally pleasant, "Why?" My husband, born and raised in the South where children either are polite or silent or both, finds these exchanges unnerving. My Italian parents, reared on the anarchist legend of Sacco and Vanzetti, are untroubled by Daniel's worldview but that is largely because they do not have to live with him.

I now wonder if this outlook, this chronic demand to know why it is mom's way or the highway is not reasonable among children born and raised in urban Alaska, where few if any relatives are around and the family hierarchy is not etched at birth. ("Cousin Caitlin gets to go first because she's the youngest.") Alaska children are steeped in freedom, solitude, independence. They need only sit still in the backseat and watch the terrain roll by to know, as perhaps no other 21st century American child can, that if you do not like the scenery before you, just travel a few miles. It will change. A lot.

I do not actually call myself a true Alaska woman. Like many frontier brides before me, I was a scared and lonely newcomer. Confronted by the strip-mall laden streets of Anchorage ("instant Albuquerque," John McPhee once called it), I was often lost. That first winter we were largely without the heavy-duty boots, heavy-duty sleeping bags, heavy-duty tires, and heavy-duty everything else that make winter bivouacs tolerable. When I tried to cross-country ski in gear that was heavy-duty in New Mexico or Utah, I froze. Walking to work some mornings in June, I would wear light cotton gloves, the liners from my winter mittens, to keep my hands warm.

After all these summers, I no longer wear cotton gloves in June. I just have cold hands like everyone else.

The only person to call me a true Alaska woman is my mother, whom I never set out to write about but who figures in everything I write anyway. The last time she called me a true Alaska woman was over breakfast on a recent trip home, when I mentioned that I'd spent Memorial Day digging a half-foot deep trench for the water line of our new house.

She had mistaken a true Alaska woman—one who does not panic when the snowmachine brake cable fails but who reaches instead for a wrench—for the self-reliant woman she had taught me to be. I wanted to explain.

But conversations with my mother, now in her seventies and attending my wheelchair-bound father with no outside help, rarely provide an opening for topics other than ones she wants to discuss. Once you have caught on to this strategy it ceases to be frustrating and becomes a somewhat admirable self-protecting trait, another of my mother's skills, like canning and seamstressing, that I have never learned. "I can't imagine being you," my mother once said when I'd called home.

But I have always imagined being her. Self-disciplined, clean-living, kind but not naive, frugal, mindful of the limitations of children, not overly sentimental, and above all, self-reliant. Highly desirable traits in anyone, they are also necessary in women of Alaska's urban frontier.

"Mom," I tried to say, "I learned to be a true Alaska woman from you!" But she was already mapping out that night's dinner and the next day's round of doctor's appointments for my father between visits from the lawn guy and the air conditioning guy.

But I like to think she would have found my observation so obvious that the whole thing isn't worth another mention. At least not among women who drive carefully, laugh with children but do not coddle them, often skip dessert and are not overly sentimental.

Between true Alaskan women like us, the obvious goes un-said. ✒

❧

Just like humans, airplanes need exercise. Going out for a spin regularly rids them of the cobwebs collected during the winter's inactivity. So, that's why my father, Hank, and I had ventured out to Lake Hood on that cold winter day.

Megan Rust

The Hard Way Out

*There is no easy exit from a Super Cub
fallen through the ice*

by Megan Rust

The day detailed in "The Hard Way Out" might have
been the day lifelong Alaskan Megan Rust decided
to become a professional pilot herself. She was
well into that flying career when a severe head
injury crushed her dreams. Unable to return to the
sky, she created an alter ego to fly for her: Taylor
Morgan, protagonist of her Alaskan mediflight
mystery series, has appeared in three books,
Dead Stick, Red Line, and *Coffin Corner,* which
are available nationwide. Rust finds flying as
Morgan is a wonderful way to experience her love
of aviation without even having to climb out of
her pajamas. ๛

"UP YOU GO," FATHER BARKED, lifting me into the Super
Cub's passenger's seat, just behind where the pilot sits in
the cockpit. My yellow snowsuit crinkled as he dropped me
into my perch. He wiggled into the front of the
compartment, burying me under his heavy parka as he
clambered into place and checked my seat belt. Then, he
secured his own. With a throaty snarl, the Cub's engine
started easily when he engaged it.

If I had known the afternoon would end with me staring
at the underside of a sheet of lake ice, I would have worn
something different.

In November 1965 I accompanied my pilot father to
Anchorage's Lake Hood to fly his 1957 Piper Super Cub. Both
the plane and I were eight years old then—I'm a 1957 model,
too. But with its striking red-and-mustard-gold paint scheme,
the Super Cub was prettier than I was.

Just like humans, airplanes need exercise. Going out for
a spin regularly rids them of the cobwebs collected during
the winter's inactivity. So, that's why my father, Hank, and
I had ventured out to Lake Hood on that cold winter day.
The temperature hovered around zero, or slightly below.

I trailed behind my father as he went to prepare N4361A
for departure. He'd parked it out on the raw ice of Lake Hood.
During the summer, Lake Hood acted as a base for numerous
seaplanes. During the winter it served ski-equipped planes.
Three or four other aircraft were parked next to it—painted
tomato red, emergency-flasher-yellow, or blue-and-gold—but
no activity surrounded them. Their owners had the sense to
stay home in front of a crackling fire.

I was extremely pleased by my dad's invitation to fly with
him, and the weather added to my delight. The sky was a
bright, cloudless blue. The sun beamed down on us, trying to
trick us into thinking it was actually warm.

First, Father unwrapped the insulated cover from the Super
Cub's engine. The cowling was cocooned like a caterpillar inside
the bright, red nylon wrap until he dragged it off and exposed
the plane's nose to the cold. If an inanimate object could shiver,
the Cub's teeth were chattering when it was stripped of its
long underwear.

Dad unplugged and removed the heater from its perch inside the cowling. The bright orange extension cord that had supplied juice to the heater needed to be re-coiled, so I did my part by wrapping the stiff plastic line around my forearm and laying the loops on a white snow berm. My dad removed the frost-coated nylon wing covers and windshield cover. My breath clouded above my head like cartoon dialogue balloons as I stamped my feet to warm them. Inside his lined gloves, his cold-soaked fingers ached as he fumbled with the knotted rope that tethered the Cub to cables frozen into the ice.

Once we took our places in the aircraft, he started the engine. With a short burst of power, the Super Cub edged away from its tie-down spot, and we maneuvered across the ice. The engine needed to be completely warm before take-off, so Father intended to taxi until it was ready to go.

I was peering out the side window as we taxied, enthralled by my first airplane ride and my dad's command of such a powerful machine. The cold of 1965 had created a very sturdy sheet of ice over the lake, and Father had no reason to be cautious while he taxied across it. He never would have placed the plane on the lake in the first place if he hadn't trusted its thickness.

Unfortunately, though, that year something unusual had happened. A warm spring had appeared, gurgling up from the bottom of the lake, hidden from view. The higher temperature of the spring water was enough to thin the ice, but not hot enough to melt it and its snow covering. That would have warned my father of the danger, and he would have steered clear.

Instead, he taxied right across it. With a sickening crack and shudder, the ice sheet below us caved in and the Super Cub plunged into the frigid water.

Father had no warning. The skis kept us afloat for only a moment before they began to bubble below the surface.

Only a second passed before Father began to free us from the sinking plane. Grabbing at the clip to unfasten his harness — hampered by bulky winter clothing and cramped quarters inside the small plane — he tore at it. Once it disconnected, he twisted in his seat to free me from my own restraints. Terrified,

I gaped out the window where the water lapped at the fuselage.

The struggle with our seat belts took many precious seconds, and when he shoved the Super Cub's clamshell door open, water surged into the cabin. The piercing sensation of glacial water hitting my skin took my breath away. I felt like I was sitting on a melting Popsicle. The plane was sinking rapidly.

When Father dragged himself out onto the Super Cub's ski, he was up to his chest in water and the plane was wallowing in it. It continued to sink, the bottom of the lake still another ten feet below it. He pulled me out of the cockpit, too, and I dropped into deepening water barely above thirty-two degrees.

The weight of our winter clothes, water-soaked and cumbersome, further reduced our mobility. By that time, we were choking and gasping in dark liquid, trying to hold our breath in a lake full of stirred-up debris and mud. I paddled frantically to reach the water clear of ice, coughing and hacking as I flapped. The murk nearly hid the bright colors of the fuselage, and the temperature of the water made my teeth ache.

As the fuselage sank, the wings began to block the break in the ice created when the plane fell through. No hole was left in the solid ice, and we were trapped below. There was no way out.

We needed some kind of battering ram to break through the ice, but we had nothing. Father knew beating on the ice with our hands was not going to work. We were running out of air.

Then he had an idea.

Father grabbed me by the legs and shoved me, head first, through the ice sheet! We had our battering ram. My skull pierced the thin ice like a plow truck's snow blade. He boosted me out of the water, up onto the wing and safety, as I snorted and spat slimy lake water out of my mouth. His adult weight was too much for the fragile ice, and he broke through quite a bit of it before obtaining a hold and climbing onto the wing.

As we struggled to extricate ourselves from the frigid waters of Lake Hood, aircraft mechanics working nearby spotted us. They stretched a ladder across the ice. My dad and I struggled onto it and headed for the shore on our hands and knees.

Once we reached terra firma, the other people rushed us into a warm hangar. They stripped us of our wet clothes and wrapped us in Army blankets. Even the scratchiness of the olive-drab fabric felt good on my chilled skin. A cup of hot, black coffee was forced down my protesting throat.

We were safe.

"What was the worst part of your ordeal?" you may ask. "When you fell through? The water of Lake Hood choking your life away? The blow to your head when your dad thrust you through the ice?"

"Nope," I would reply. "It was that coffee. To this day, I don't drink the stuff. I shiver just thinking about it." ❧

◈

It had taken me thirty-one years getting to this point: catching my first fish. Everything that brought me to standing on a drift boat engaged in battle with a fish flashed through my head.

Stacey Saunders

Fishing: A Love Story

The making of a sports fishing fanatic

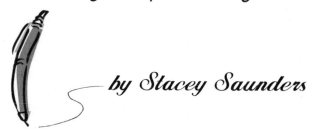

by Stacey Saunders

Stacey Saunders was born in Akron, Ohio. She received a B.A. in English and Spanish from Concordia College in Moorhead, Minnesota. After graduating from Valparaiso University School of Law in Indiana, she fled the glut of 1980s law school graduates to seek work in Alaska. Her tourism articles for *Alaska Business Monthly* magazine have allowed her to learn more about her adopted home state and write about it. Stacey is ecstatic to write pieces without old Latin phrases and sentences beginning "Whereas. . . ." She lives in Anchorage with her husband Michael and dog Odo. ❧

SOMETHING SLAMMED THE END OF MY LINE as if it was trying to jerk the pole from my hand.

So that's a king salmon, I thought.

"Pump up!" said Mark, our fishing guide. I held my pole straight up. "Everyone else reel your lines in." Mark didn't want their lines to cross mine. My pole's tip bowed slightly and the reel began to hiss and spin. "That's right, let 'im run." Suddenly, the taut line went slack and quiet. "Reel down!" Gripping the pole tightly in my left hand, I cranked the handle with my right; it was awkward for a lefty. A silver tail flashed up from the river. My king was an expert at tug-of-war. I pumped and reeled on Mark's command, bracing the end of the pole between my knees for leverage. My arm muscles shook with fatigue.

It had taken me thirty-one years getting to this point: catching my first fish. Everything that brought me to standing on a drift boat engaged in battle with a fish flashed through my head.

When I was five, I went fishing with my father and grandfather. I don't remember where we went nor what kind of fish we were after. I grew up in Akron, Ohio. My father was a meticulously dressed architect who played with a jazz trio on weekends. But he also loved hunting, raising beagles, and fishing. One day he said I was going fishing with him and his father. I was excited. Daddy and Papa stood in the water while I was propped in my child-sized lawn chair with a small pole and a plastic worm for bait. I waited patiently, but no fish. Daddy found me slumped and nodding in my chair. He lifted me into the truck and opened the sack lunch Mom packed for me. Big pink frosted animal cookies for dessert. It was the perfect day. We got home after dark, but I was allowed to stay up to eat some of the fish my grandmother fried. Mom, my aunt, uncles and cousins crowded into the kitchen, eating and laughing. That was the first and last time my father and I went fishing. He died four years later when I was nine.

For years after his death, my mother and other adults talked about wanting a male relative or friend to take my younger brother fishing. No one talked about taking me fishing. After all, I was a girl and none of the other little Black girls I knew fished. We were expected to play with dolls, stay clean, and do the "hair thing." Young Black girls in the 1960s weren't necessarily judged by weight, but everyone seemed to have an opinion about your hair. It went beyond style. Hair was a social and political statement. Whether you wore your hair "natural" or "straightened" was taken as an expression of how — or if — you wanted to be accepted by members of the opposite race. It was a lot of pressure and came at a high price in terms of expense, discomfort and time.

Other kids feared dentists but I was afraid of hairdressers. To have presentable hair for church and school, we had the choice of facing hot pressing irons or smelly permanents. Stinky perms were followed by huge plastic rollers pinned to my scalp as I roasted under a hot dryer. Saturday morning hair appointments interfered with cartoons and playing outside.

"Don't get that hair wet!" was the parental mantra every little girl in my Sunday school class heard. We learned to avoid rain, humidity, swimming pools, sweaty sports, squirt gun fights. I heard a comedian say "water to a Black woman is like kryptonite to Superman." Fear of a bad hair day and lack of athletic ability turned me into an indoor bookworm. Two Girl Scout camping trips and one summer at my grandmother's Bible camp were the extent of my outdoor education.

College and law school took me from Ohio to Virginia, Minnesota and Indiana. In the South, I never fit in with the girls in designer jeans, pumps and elaborate hairdos. In my junior year, I transferred to a college in northern Minnesota. In this college town, I was regarded as exotic since I wasn't Norwegian or Finnish. What I looked like started to matter less. For transportation I bought a ten-speed Raleigh and christened it "Sir Walter, the." But the closest I came to an extreme sport was a forty-five minute walk in minus forty degree weather to take my LSAT. Law school in a small town in Indiana allowed little time for anything beyond heavy course loads, and shoveling snow.

In the 1980s, it seemed that every other person was a law school graduate. From opposite ends of the country, Michael, now my husband, and I arrived in Alaska — not seeking pristine scenery, great adventures, or soul mates, but jobs. In Alaska, we found work, each other and much more.

For the first ten years we lived our lives like we would have if we had lived in any medium-sized city in the Lower 48. That was until we met our fishing fairy godmothers, Char and Barbara.

Char, a serene massage therapist, and frontierswoman, lived in Talkeetna, a former mining and trapping town two and a half hours drive north of Anchorage. While she massaged away my work stress, she told me about taking her kids fishing and hiking when they were young. It made being outdoors sound fun and not intimidating like it did when other friends and acquaintances talked. I confided our cluelessness about doing things outdoors. She peered over her reading glasses and declared, "You guys have got to come up and go fishing with me in Talkeetna!" So thirty years after that fishing trip with my dad and grandfather, I found myself on a river bank with a reel in my hand. In our holiday newsletter, I wrote about my first fishing trip.

Christmas Letter 1995: We fished in Talkeetna on Michael's birthday. It was a beautiful Sunday drive with fall colors starting. We hoped to catch silver salmon but didn't catch anything meaningful and will exact our revenge on the river next summer. Stacey will get a pole with a left handed reel; this is one sport where she is not ambidextrous.

Char apologized during the entire drive back to her cabin. "I just don't understand! We always catch fish there!" She looked distraught, as though she had let us down.

"Don't worry about it, Char. I spent my birthday exactly the way I wanted," said Michael. We agreed to go back and try again the following year.

Christmas Letter 1996: We went fishing for silvers again on Michael's birthday weekend.

We did not mention how a stomach virus nearly ended the trip before it even started. Michael dragged himself to work the entire week before the trip. "If you don't stay home and get better," I said, "you're not going this weekend." We compromised. He attended a settlement conference from bed with the hand-held phone tucked under his chin as I forced liquids and crackers on him. By the weekend, he was back on solid food, and we set off for Talkeetna.

Char arranged for a charter to drop us at one of her favorite spots. She brought her five-year-old grandson Jesse, who was thrilled to fish with grownups. It took five or six trips to unload everything from the boat to the dock: sleeping bags, tents, coolers of food, Coleman stove, lanterns, and fishing gear. Other boat passengers helped us unload by passing everything forward.

"Gee, how long are you going to be camping?" a man in a baseball cap asked.

"Overnight." Michael said. Everyone doubled over laughing.

"Aunt Char always takes everything," said the boat's driver, who was one of her teenage nephews.

On the dock at our drop-off point about forty minutes later, we found several abandoned cabins. Char said the property had been condemned and the owners simply left the cabins where they were. One had a broken window, but the roof was intact. We decided to stay there instead of setting up our tents. Michael and I had brought breakfast foods, but Char had brought huge thick steaks, potatoes, freshly ground coffee, and cold beer.

"Char! This is great, but you're spoiling us!" said Michael.

"I wanted you guys to come up and relax. I'll cook after we get some fishing in," she said.

"Did you guys pick up bait?" Char asked, peering into paper sacks on the cabin steps.

"Yeah," I answered sitting down. I was starting to feel pain in my lower stomach. "Michael, where's the bag I asked you to hold in the car?" Michael paused and looked at me.

"In the car," he finally answered, turning away and staring at the cabin floor.

"Michael!" I was feeling sick by now, and not just over missing bait.

"It's OK! It's OK!" Char soothed, picking up her cell phone. "Hey, you guys, it's Char. When's the next boat coming up? Can you bring some bait. . ." She turned and saw me grab a roll of toilet paper from a duffle bag and dash for the woods, "And some Pepto Bismol?"

I ran toward an outhouse I had seen two hundred feet from our cabin. The door was nailed shut. Stomach flu in the forest. This is going to be a miserable weekend, I thought, heading for some bushes. Michael stood guard with his back turned. Now I was sick and depressed. I might not get to fish at all. When the next boat dropped off people and our replacement bait, I could take the boat back to Talkeetna. But there would be nowhere to stay until the end of the day. I was too weak to drive back to Char's. No, staying in the cabin made more sense. Michael, Char, and Jesse could still fish. Michael would feel guilty about leaving me behind in the cabin and stop fishing to come back to check on me. His trip and his birthday would be ruined. But I decided to stick it out.

As we walked inside, Char held up a paper sack containing bait and stomach medicine. I swallowed the thick pink liquid and settled onto my sleeping bag while Char set up the camp stove. Michael and Jesse chatted with some passing fishermen and then followed them to the river.

I woke up two hours later and felt better. Three men who looked like they were in their twenties were talking to Char and Michael. The men held bulging green garbage bags and said they had "limited out." Fishing fever vanquished the rest of my queasiness. I pulled on my hip waders, and we all began to trudge through the woods to a fishing hole that the three young men said was "hot." Nothing was going to stop me from catching a fish. It didn't need to be the "Big One." I was humbled by the forgotten bait and my earlier nature call in the woods. I sloshed a hundred feet from the cabin and suddenly found myself face first on the ground. Lesson number ninety-nine: Rubber waders aren't solid footing on wet grass or mud. Char unkinked my neck and back as soon as I got up.

"Boy, I didn't even see you go down! I was talking to Jesse, and when I turned around, you'd disappeared!" Michael said.

"Yeah, well, no more bad luck. Let's get some fish!" I slogged through the mud, hanging onto my pole, my balance, and the rest of my pride.

I watched Char bundling clumps of tiny red salmon eggs into black net squares. She was baiting our hooks. "Show me how, Char." I asked. I figured she'd pampered us enough. Char looked at my hands and hesitated.

"It's really slimy and your nails. . ." A reformed nail-biter, I'd grown them long and painted them red.

"So, they'll wash off. If the polish chips, I'll touch up when I get home." She showed me how to arrange the bait onto the sharp hooks. I cast several times and had to replace the eggs every few casts. I felt guilty using so much bait. Still no fish. Then late afternoon, the fishing gods had mercy.

During our last two hours on the river, five-year-old Jesse handed his pole to his grandmother and wedged himself into a space behind me on the bank where I fished. He soon fell asleep with his head on my back. My mind drifted to blankness as I listened to his breathing and matched its rhythm to the ripples in the water. Suddenly, I felt a tug on the line and reeled in, calling to Char and Michael, "Fish on!"

Jesse woke up and jumped down from behind me to take a look.

"Hey Stacey, that's a nice one." Char said wading over to me. It was a rainbow trout.

"Yeah, not bad for my first fish ever," I said, holding the line as Char cut it. Relief. I would not go home empty-handed. I held up the trout to Michael. "Dinner!"

Michael hugged me. "Good job, kid!"

Back in Anchorage, we pan-fried the trout for Michael's birthday dinner. I had recovered enough to eat some of it. "Next year, salmon!" We grinned and toasted his birthday.

Christmas Letter 1996: Michael estimated that Stacey's trout cost us $70 per pound.

Our circle of friends grew. Alaskans seemed particularly open to "I have a cousin whose ex-wife's next door neighbor is coming on a cruise next summer. I gave him your number. Maybe you can get together for dessert." Our second fishing fairy godmother Barbara, a tart-tongued, chain smoking nurse, had been saying for some time we needed to fish with her on the Kasilof with her friend Mark.

"Trout?" Reading our annual letter, Barbara was unimpressed. "You two are coming with me!" The high priestess of salmon fishing had spoken. We'd met Mark and his wife Maggie at a party and liked them. Mark operated a guide service on the Kasilof River. The Kasilof is less crowded than the larger Russian and Kenai Rivers. The entire Kenai Peninsula is considered some of North America's best sportfishing. Unlike Char's idea of fishing as a relaxing, leisurely pastime under blue skies surrounded by lush green forests, for Barbara, fishing, like war, is hell. She fishes on Mark's boat several times a year.

"We need to be on the river by 10:00. So, Katie (one of Barbara's roommates) and I will pick you up at 5:00 A.M. Sharp! Be ready, bring warm clothes and something to drink. I'll bring tuna salad. We're going to have sooo much fun!" Barbara did not breathe between sentences as she issued final orders.

At 4:50 A.M. Katie and Barbara picked us up. Barbara had worked a late shift at the hospital, so Katie drove Barbara's car. Michael sat up front chatting with her. I sat in the back with Barbara, who fell asleep an hour into the trip. When we pulled onto Mark and Maggie's property, Barbara sat up, ready to go. We reached the boat launch and saw other guides taking drift boats with three and four passengers out onto the Kasilof.

Barbara and Katie settled in the front of the boat, Michael and I behind them, and Mark rowed. After dropping anchor, Mark baited our hooks and then patiently showed Michael and me how to cast and how the line felt when kings bite. Hours passed. The sun beat down on us. I concentrated so hard that I could scarcely see my line in the water. I gazed up at the bald eagles nesting in trees along the bank. Then Katie's line jerked. Wordlessly, she reeled it in. Barbara's forehead creased, and she grimaced as she watched Mark scoop Katie's thrashing king into the net. He hit it with a wooden bat until it stopped wriggling.

"Kinda red, isn't it?" Barbara sniped at her housemate, glaring into the net. We knew that red meant it was not as fresh as one which was "silver" in color.

"Are you saying your salmon is lovelier than mine?" Katie asked.

"I didn't get one yet!" Barbara shot back.

"I didn't think so!" Katie posed with her fish as I snapped pictures.

Settling into my seat, I picked up my pole in my left hand and flicked an eyelash out my eye with my right. At that moment, everyone in our boat and the one next to us began to shout at me. "You've got one! You've got one! Set the hook, Stacey!"

It was gone in an instant, and I hadn't felt a thing.

"You can always scratch your eye later," Michael said.

"Thank you very much, Mr. I-Had-Three-Kings-on-the-Line-Last Week-and-Lost-Them!"

Mark came up and knelt between our seats. Tall and powerfully built, he barely fit. Mark looked from Michael to me, cupped his hands together like a new age guru, and said in a soothing voice, "I'm here for you both." The combination of his baseball cap, t-shirt and earnest television marriage-counselor/therapist expression was too much. We all shrieked with laughter.

About ten minutes later, Barbara caught a king. She posed for a photo with her fish, then, like a diva ending a successful concert settled into her seat, size five waders stretched out over the bow. She lit a cigarette and fluffed her curly blond hair as she blew smoke rings into the sky. All was well.

Only Michael and I were still salmon-less. Then five minutes after Barbara's victory, I got my second hit. I was not going to lose this one. So even as my arms throbbed, I kept reeling with my right hand, feeling like a dork.

"Gettin' tired, Stacey?" Michael said.

"She's all right. She's doing fine," Mark said.

Just when I thought I couldn't hold on any longer, Mark said, "Ok, Stacey, now keep your tip low and swing him back this way toward me." He held a net that looked like the kind mad scientists in the movies use to chase butterflies. "Easy, easy. Hold it. Now swing out and bring it toward me." I swayed my line to the right as Mark brought the net up under a big silvery, thrashing fish.

He thumped it with the gaff. "Wow, Stacey, that's a beauty. Michael, give me the camera." Barbara reached behind her as my husband pulled the camera from my backpack. I squealed and pumped my fist. I remembered being five, on the bank with Daddy and Papa. They were laughing and cheering each other as they reeled in fish after fish. I felt I had arrived.

Many kings, reds, and silvers later, fishing has become an established part of our summer routine. I keep a box of "fishing clothes" so I can leave in an hour's notice when Barbara calls and says "Want to go fishing?" My box includes hair clippies and a baseball cap. I stopped worrying about my hair and looking bad during a rainy trip for reds. In honor of my progress from fishing-impaired to fisher-woman, Barbara gave me a t-shirt that reads: "Reel Women Never Lie About the Size."

Sometimes Michael and I fish together and sometimes we engage in extramarital fishing. We've learned to accept getting skunked once in a while.

At Barbara's annual St. Patrick's Day party, Mark and Maggie announced they were building a website for their guide service and that it included a photo of us with our salmon. "What's the caption," I said, "'If these people can catch fish, anyone can?'"

So, when do the new fishing licenses go on sale? ✍

◦ら

That winter we ran out of meat
and had to take a deer out of
season, a doe. She was fat,
with thick, shining brown hide,
long, strong, graceful legs, a soft,
brown nose and neat little hooves.
We hung her by her back legs
from the boom and spread a tarp
to catch the guts. Her big brown
eyes stared at the deck.

Dana Stabenow

The Gift

Growing up on a 75-foot fish tender in the Gulf of Alaska

by Dana Stabenow

Dana Stabenow is the author of nineteen novels
and the Alaska Traveler column in *Alaska*
magazine, as well as various short stories, essays,
and the occasional vitriolic guest editorial in the
Anchorage Daily News. She co-hosts "Book Talk
Alaska," a monthly radio book club of the air on
Alaska Public Radio, and is an explorer for Alaska
Magazine Television. She can be reached through
her website [www.stabenow.com].

WHAT WAS IT LIKE, living on a boat? people ask me now, but when you're a kid, your life is just your life. We lived on a boat, so what? I slept in a bunk instead of a bed, I ate at a galley table instead of a kitchen nook, I played in a focsle instead of a front yard. I climbed a ladder to get to school instead of taking a bus. If it was low tide, it was a forty-two foot climb up that ladder, with barnacles at the bottom and ice at the top. If it was high tide, I could step from the deck to the dock. I loved high tide, although low tide had its good points. During the long low tide climb, I occasionally lost my grip on what I carried with me, which was sometimes my homework.

We lived on a boat for five years, from the time I was in the third grade, because my mother was a deckhand on a seventy-five foot salmon tender called the Celtic. We lived on board most of that time. She referred to me as supercargo. I thought that meant excess baggage, but when I looked it up years later in Webster's I found, "a merchant-ship officer who is in charge of the cargo and the commercial concerns of the voyage." There was the skipper, the deckhand and me, the supercargo. I think now she was trying to make me feel like I had a place on board, a title and duties to go with them.

Most Alaskans love the beginning of summer. So do I. I didn't then. It meant leaving Seldovia, leaving all my friends, leaving solid land behind for another three months on the water. It meant maintenance. The Celtic was an old boat with a wooden hull, and every spring she was put into dry dock so we could scrape the hull free of barnacles and kelp and paint it with copper paint. The copper in the paint discouraged wood-eating worms from burrowing in and chowing down. You haven't lived until you've had to grow copper paint out of your hair.

When the salmon hit Cook Inlet, the fishing boats hit it with them, and the Celtic was not far behind. We went wherever the fishing boats had nets in the water. We would offload groceries and fresh water and parts and fuel, and load fish. The skipper sat in the galley writing fish tickets. My mother stood on the catwalk outside the wheelhouse, five silver counters on each hand. One hand kept count of the fish loaded from the boat to starboard, the other from the boat to port.

There was one counter for each kind of fish: kings, reds, silvers, humpies and dogs. I never learned the difference between reds and silvers. The humpies I knew because they were little, three pounds, and the dogs because they were big, eight to ten. The kings were biggest, thirty pounds and up. Mom knew them all, on sight, from thirty feet. I can still see her there, looking down from the catwalk, forearms resting on the railing, fingers moving swiftly and accurately on their many counters. She was as dark as I was fair, with brown hair, brown eyes and an olive skin that tanned easily in the constant glare of an Arctic summer sun. She would look up and see me staring, and her teeth would flash white in a quick smile. You okay, honey? she'd ask. I'm okay, Mom, I'd say. You catching all those strays? Every one, Mom.

Mom would take the deckboards off the hold and brace them to form a slide between the gunnel and the opening of the hold. The fishermen pewed their fish up over the side of the Celtic and, theoretically, the fish would hit the slide and slip right into the hold. In practice, about one in five of the salmon slid to the deck, where I stood with my own pew, ready to snag strays. A pew in my nine-year-old hands with a couple of reds on the other end formed a pretty effective counterweight. One day I got cocky and pewed up three salmon. I staggered over to the hold, confident that Mom's admiring eyes were upon me, and tilted the pew. The salmon didn't slide off the single prong like they were supposed to, I didn't let go of the wooden handle like I should have and all of us ended up in the hold together. There were already a lot of salmon in the hold so I landed soft. They fished me out when they stopped laughing. I can laugh about it, too. Now.

I didn't eat salmon again until I was thirty-five. On the Celtic it got into everything whether you fell in it or not. There were fish scales on my clothes, in my hair, on my pillow. The water from the head and galley taps smelled like fish. The deck, no matter how hard we scrubbed it down, retained a faint, slippery layer of gurry. Mom's special homemade maple syrup (one cup of water, one cup of brown sugar, one teaspoon of maple flavoring) tasted of fish. Far enough into the fishing season, we stopped taking showers because stale sweat smelled better than stale fish.

The chartroom behind the wheelhouse and above the galley was my room. At Mom's request, the skipper cut a hole in the floor and constructed a sliding door so I could shinny down without having to use one of the two outside ladders on the port and starboard sides of the cabin. The head of the bunk was right next to the chart table, with rolled charts of Cook Inlet and Prince William Sound and the Barren Islands and Kodiak and Shelikof Strait stacked in a slatted shelf hanging from the overhead. I used to pull them down one at a time and plan imaginary voyages to those mysterious seas and lands beyond the edge of the map. I could look up and out the window and stare at that edge, a rolling expanse of endless water, gray in winter, green in summer, blue in sunshine, no finite end to it or to my imaginings as to what lay beyond it. Kids with trees in their front yards instead of belugas, I bet. Here There Be Dragons, indeed.

We saw our share of belugas, and pilot whales and orcas and humpbacks. One trip the fog came down like a white, wet blanket, and the fathometer went out. We shut down the engines so we could listen for the surf to tell us when we were getting too close to the beach. A baby gray whale surfaced right next to us, blew spume over the starboard gunnel, and spent the next half hour surfacing and diving and blowing all around us. Mom said he thought we were his mother.

There were other fish in the sea. One summer in Tuxedni Bay, we were at anchor while the fleet went fishing. Mom saw a boat being pulled out of the bay. A gigantic halibut had managed to tangle itself up in the boat's net, and it was towing the gear and the boat and the fishermen, too, right out of the bay and against the tide at that. We had to grapple onto the fishing boat, swing the boom over, hook the tackle around the corkline and use the winch to hoist the gear and the halibut onto the deck of the Celtic. It was so big we had to shoot it before we brought it on board or it would have beat the boat to pieces. It took four shots. When it was freed from the net, the halibut's nose was poking into the focsle door while its tail was bent against the galley bulkhead. We didn't have a scale big enough to weigh it. Mom said it had to be at least four hundred pounds.

When we butchered it out, the heart was still beating. Mom put it on the stern gunnel and it was still beating that night when I went to bed. It was still beating the next morning when I got up, beating slowly but thump-thump, thump-thump, thump-thump, there it was. I had nightmares for weeks afterward. The halibut cheeks were great, though, especially as we'd been eating salmon for a month straight.

Another time we were sick of salmon we went on shore and harvested some immature seagulls. We plucked and cleaned the birds and Mom simmered them in a Dutch oven all afternoon. Five minutes after she set the pot out on the foredeck to cool, the Fish and Game landed in a float plane and taxied up for a visit. We could have been fined and jailed, not to mention the boat confiscated; seagulls are legally protected as organic garbage disposals. The skipper was petrified. Mom invited the fish hawk to stay for dinner. He did. If he knew, he didn't say anything, although I don't see how he could have missed all those seagull feathers floating off the stern.

Whenever my mom spotted a sea otter, she would haul me up to the bridge so I could see it. I didn't mind because they were so cute, and because it didn't happen very often. At that time the Alaskan sea otter was almost gone. Mom explained to me how the Russian-America Company had forced the Aleuts to hunt sea otters so the fur could be shipped to Europe and made into coats and hats. The Russian-America Company had no thought of conservation, only of commerce, and two hundred years later they were only just beginning to return to the Gulf of Alaska. We should bear witness, Mom said. I didn't know what she meant, then.

If you're out on the water enough, pretty soon you run into a storm, and the Celtic stood up to her share. I remember coming around Port Dick one October during one storm, the worst I can remember. On Mom's orders I lay in a stateroom below, watching through the porthole next to the bunk. First all dense, dark green water through the round, thick glass, then all dense, dark gray clouds, then all water, then all clouds, hard aport, hard astarboard the boat heeled, over and over again, hours and hours of it. I gripped the sides of the bunk in both hands to keep from being thrown to the floor.

The wind would gust, pushing the bow off course and cross-wise of an oncoming wave. The hull would rise up and slam down, rise up, slam down. Water crashed over the bow and poured down over the foredeck and the cabin, sluicing out of the holes in the gunnels only to make way for the next wave. We were as much under the water as we were on top of it most of the time. The only good news was that I was too scared to be seasick.

We ran into Picnic Harbor at daybreak the next morning. Although my mother never admitted to the danger, I noticed she was as glad as I was to gain the safety of that long, narrow, serene little bay, rimmed with dark green spruce and spindly, leafless birch, and the comforting bulk of the Kenai Mountains looming up behind. Terra firma. Firm land. I have always loved the sound of that phrase.

Mom taught me how to steer a compass heading, moving one spoke of the wheel at a time, watching the bow for the course correction, another spoke, another wait. Seventy-five foot boats don't exactly turn on a dime, but once they start turning they don't dilly-dally, either. You don't want to over-steer and wind up hard aground on Point Pogibshi, Mom said.

Once I saw her dock the Celtic alone. We were in port at the fuel dock, and the skipper had disappeared uptown to the nearest bar. We had to move because there were other boats waiting to fuel up. My arms were too short to reach around the piling, and I was too little anyway to handle one-inch manila line. The best I could do was stay out of the way. Mom pulled in the bow line, climbed the ladder to the wheelhouse and started the engine. With it in neutral, she banged out of the wheelhouse, slid down the ladder and raced back to free the stern line.

She ran back up the deck, climbed up to the wheelhouse and put the engine in gear just as the bow was beginning to drift away from the dock. She put the throttle at just enough above idle to generate forward motion. When we got close to our new mooring, she threw the engine into neutral, banged back out of the wheelhouse, down the ladder and hit the stern just about the time the dock was sliding by it. She slapped the stern line around a piling and the eye over a cleat. She ran back up the deck, up the ladder, into the wheelhouse, put the engine into reverse, brought the bow back from where it had strayed, put the engine back into neutral, slammed out of the wheelhouse, down the ladder, up to the bow just in time to slap the bow line around the piling before it slipped out of reach, and back to the wheelhouse to shut down the engine.

That was the first time I remember thinking, my mom can do anything.

Including shoot. With twenty-ten vision she was the best shot on the boat. She insisted I learn how to use a gun, too, and bought me a little twenty-two rifle. We'd go ashore once a week so I could plink away at Blazo cans. Pull the stock in tight against your shoulder, she'd say, sight down the barrel to the little bead on the end, breathe out and hold it, squeeze the trigger, don't jerk. I was always a lousy shot, and I hated loud noises besides, but she was very firm. What if something happened to her? I had to know how to take care of myself. That included learning how to shoot, how to build a fire, if I was lost how to follow a creek downstream to another, bigger creek, that creek downstream to a river and that river to civilization.

We hunted moose from the Celtic, anchoring in Kamishak Bay and rowing to shore. The best year ever was when we got a moose right on the beach. None of us could believe it, no fighting the mosquitoes, no butchering in a swamp, no packing it out in pieces through miles of brush. I had blood up to my eyebrows, and I loved every minute of it because all I had to do was haul my share ten feet to the water's edge, dump it in the skiff, and go back for more.

We hunted ducks there, too; it was the first time Mom used a shotgun. We took the skiff into a nearby salt marsh, Mom sitting on a midships thwart, facing the stern, holding a double-barreled twelve gauge at the ready. I was watching from the bow. A flock of ducks exploded into the sky and she pulled the shotgun in tight and fired. The force of the blast knocked her into a backwards somersault that landed her head right between my feet. She blinked up at me, and when she got her breath back we both burst out laughing. She got two ducks, though. We had them for dinner, plucked, stuffed and roasted.

One winter we trapped mink and marten in Prince William Sound, on Montague and Knight Islands. We found blueberries as big as my thumb, and Mom made blueberry syrup, blueberry jelly, blueberry pancakes, blueberry quickbread. We had to walk the trapline twice a week, and once there was a mink still alive in a trap. We shot him, and he was so shiny and pretty I volunteered to carry him back—a mistake, because he smelled worse than the bottom of an outhouse in July. They smell that way in nature, Mom said, and did not volunteer to take him from me. I see women wearing mink coats now and I think, if you only knew.

That winter we ran out of meat and had to take a deer out of season, a doe. She was fat, with thick, shining brown hide, long, strong, graceful legs, a soft, brown nose and neat little hooves. We hung her by her back legs from the boom and spread a tarp to catch the guts. Her big brown eyes stared at the deck. I started to cry. Mom reached around me and closed the eyes with a gentle hand, and after that it was better.

One fall night we were headed for port after a successful moose hunt in Kamishak. It was a clear night; you could see all the way to the edge of the universe and round back to the other side. Nothing disturbed the surface of the water but our wake. Mom was on watch, and I stood next to her as she taught me the constellations: Orion first, the Big and Little Dippers, Cassiopeia. She set the autopilot and we went out on the catwalk so she could show me how to find Polaris. I saw a falling star. Quick, make a wish, Mom said, and I did, closing my eyes, opening them again to see another falling star and another and another. I remembered Henny Penny. The sky is falling, Mom, I said. It's a meteor shower, she said. We stayed out there for an hour, watching the sky fall, its image reflected in the ebony mirror below.

I grew up believing I could do anything because my mother showed me how. She could bake bread, shoot and skin and butcher a moose, shoot, pluck and cook ducks, help maintain and run a boat, count fish, fool the Fish and Game, skin a mink and tan its hide, homeschool me the year we trapped. She could upholster furniture, sew clothes, knit sweaters, plant gardens, work as a waitress, a slimer, a canner, a bookkeeper, ground support for an air taxi, and survive three disastrous marriages. The only thing I can remember her fearing was the thought of owing money. I watched her fill out a credit application once with her hand trembling so badly she could barely print her own name.

It is the years on the boat I remember best, though, and my mother moving through them, confident, competent, strong, always ready with a laugh and a hand to finish the job, whatever it was. Because she could do anything, I could, too.

It was her gift to me. ✍

❦

I stared in fear at the water level. It was much higher than normal due to all the rain we'd had. Heavy foam appeared at each dip in the river. The roar of the water was so loud we had to shout to be heard.

Deb Wahrer

If You Ain't Scared You Ain't Having Fun

Not everyone's into river rafting.
Some aren't even in the raft

by Deb Wahrer

Deborah Wahrer lives in Anchorage with her husband Roger and their two cats. After twenty years working in the Alaska oil industry, she quit her job in order to study creative writing, graduating in 1998. Despite her rafting experience, Deborah continues to try new outdoor activities—and continues to fall into rivers, down mountains, and over boulders. She is currently writing a suspense novel.⤚

"HOW THE HELL did she talk me into this?" I asked myself for the hundredth time. I was hanging on for dear life as the raft catapulted down the river. At times, the raft hit the water with such force it tossed me into the air.

If only I'd stuck to my guns when Judy called to invite me on her annual rafting trip. I had known it was coming up and had promised myself I wouldn't be pressured into going again.

It's not that I'd had a miserable time the year before. It had been a sunny day, and the water had been fairly calm with only five or six mild "rapids." But Judy and her husband Bernie are pranksters, whose favorite part of the trip is getting close enough to another raft to pour water on their friends. After being on the receiving end of a bucket of cold river water, I'd decided once was enough.

Unfortunately, Judy wasn't one to take no for an answer. When I tried to get out of it by telling her I had too much to do, she said, "Oh, come on. It's just for one day. You can't be that busy." She started in on how long it had been since they'd seen me. That I never came to visit anymore. That I'd missed Bernie's forty-first birthday party. That I never seemed to want to do anything.

I got the same scolding every time I saw or talked to her. I could picture her on the other end of the phone, her short, curly brown hair bobbing up and down with each nod of her head and her hand resting on her ample hip. The speech no longer had any effect on me.

But then she got my attention by saying, "You're always such a stick in the mud."

It wasn't the first time Judy had called me that, but it bothered me because she wasn't the only person to accuse me of being unwilling to try new things. I eventually told Judy I'd go. It was the only way I could think of to end the discussion.

That would have been the end of it, but I made the mistake of mentioning the conversation to my friend, Sue, that evening when we went for a walk. "That sounds great! When is it?" she asked.

I looked at her with exasperation. I'd been complaining about how Judy tried to make me feel guilty about not spending more time with her, and Sue missed the point entirely. She looked up at me, her dark hair blowing into her face. Her skin was wind-burned from her last excursion, climbing up the side of a mountain or something. Her blue eyes laughed at me, challenging me.

When she saw my expression, she continued, "You're going, aren't you? You complain beforehand but, admit it, you always have a good time when you go out with me."

When was that, I wondered. The time Sue took me hiking up Flat Top Mountain, and I ended sliding on my behind most of the way down? Or the time she tried to teach me to cross-country ski, and I fell so many times I was bruised and sore for a week? Or the fishing trip when I'd had a bad reaction to the patch that was supposed to prevent seasickness? Or, my personal favorite, the camping trip where, after hiking ten miles straight up, I'd slipped on a rock and fell into a creek?

"You should go. It'll be fun. Can I come too?" Sue asked, certain that I'd changed my mind.

That's how I found myself, that cold morning in August, standing with twenty-four other people on the bank of the Matanuska River, an hour and a half drive north of my home in Anchorage. At least it wasn't raining, as it had almost all summer. But it wasn't bright and sunny either. The sun was a pale white ball, barely visible through a thick wall of heavy, gray clouds.

We were outfitted with overalls, rubber boots, life vests, and plastic buckets. The guides for the expedition separated us into parties of six and assigned each team to one of four rafts. The rafts were dark green inflatable boats that looked like oval doughnuts. Little rings were attached around the outer edges, and rope was threaded through each. "Grab lines," the guides told us. In the center of the raft were two cross tubes, with enough room between them for a large metal chest. A steel frame, called a rowing platform, fit over the tubes, holding the oars in place.

There was a guide for each raft. Three of them were tan, muscular college-aged boys. I tried to finagle my way into one of the hunks' groups, but I ended up in the raft piloted by an older man who appeared to be in charge. He was tall and lanky with rough, weathered skin and white hair that stuck out in unruly strands. His sharp blue eyes had a crazy, fanatical look. I tried to reassure myself it was a good thing I was in his raft; his years of experience would keep me safe. But then he started talking excitedly — with hoots and hollers — about the thrills of rafting. He ended his speech by saying, "If you ain't scared, you ain't having fun."

I nicknamed him "Wild Man" and wondered if it was too late to get out of this little expedition. I met Sue's eyes with a look that I hoped told her I was not happy. She just grinned back at me.

Besides my concern about Wild Man's judgment, I was worried we wouldn't have a smooth ride like the year before. I stared in fear at the water level. It was much higher than normal due to all the rain we'd had. Heavy foam appeared at each dip in the river. The roar of the water was so loud we had to shout to be heard.

Because the river feeds from the Matanuska Glacier, the water that wasn't churning into white rapids was grayish green with silt. The overcast sky, the rafts, our olive-green overalls and boots, and the dark shadows in the birch and spruce trees along the banks created an almost monochromatic scene. Our fluorescent orange life vests provided the only splash of color.

We were loaded into the rafts. I was in the rear of the first one with Sue and a woman named Patricia. Patricia was petite with short blond hair and a smattering of freckles across her face. She looked like a teenager, but she'd told me she had graduated from college a few months earlier and was going to get married in a couple of weeks. Three men were up front, and Wild Man sat in the center so he could row. He instructed us to hold on and bail.

I saw a look pass between Wild Man and the other guides who seemed surprised by the force of the water. After a split second of hesitation, Wild Man pushed off, shouting, "Yahoooo!"

Wild Man continued to "Yahoo!" or "Yippee!" each time the raft took a jolt. Before long he was really pissing me off. I might have enjoyed the roller coaster ride more if I had been able to foresee the drops and brace myself for the sudden pitching of the raft, but I was focused on the water surging into the boat and my futile attempts to keep it at bay. Each strong bounce hurled me to my knees or flung me into the air, causing me to spill water from my bucket back into the raft.

When Sue saw me struggling, she demonstrated how to bail. In one smooth motion, she bent down and pulled the bucket through the water as she stood back up and poured its contents over the edge. She made it look easy. Of course, Sue was using both hands, while I was limited to one because I refused to let go of the grab line.

Both my hands were frozen from the cold water, and I didn't know how much longer I could keep a grip on the bucket. I also had a sore on my palm from clutching the rope. My back hurt too, from the up-and-down motion of bailing water. "I'm not having fun yet, Judy," I muttered to myself.

Wild Man shouted "Yippee!" again, and I was tempted to throw my bucket at him. This time the turbulence flung me to the floor of the raft. On impact, I heard a loud "clank." I glanced over at Patricia. She was holding her hand to her head as though deep in thought. She was saying something, but I couldn't hear her over the roar of the water. When she lowered her hand, I saw a large welt forming on her forehead and realized she must have hit her head on the rowing platform's metal frame.

Meanwhile, Wild Man yelled at us, "Bail! Bail!" I shouted at Patricia to hold onto the rope and went back to work.

Moments later Patricia screamed, "Oh my God!" She pointed behind me, her empty bucket dangling from her wrist. I turned and saw a raft bottom side up in the river. Its passengers had been thrown into the water, and their life vests were carrying them swiftly downstream.

Sue began a lookout for anyone floating past. Wild Man called to her to get out a rescue bag, a nylon sack with a line coiled inside. Holding on to the end of the rope, Sue threw the bag, with the precision of her college softball days, to a point just beyond a woman in the water. Within seconds, the woman reached it and grabbed hold. Sue wasn't tall, but she was strong and managed to pull the woman into the raft with little help from the others. The men in the front of the raft also pulled someone in, but it took them a couple of tries with the rescue bag before they succeeded.

I kept bailing. With the others occupied by the rescues, the water level had risen halfway up the sides of the boat. Fortunately, the rapids seemed to be smoothing out, and I was finally able to make some headway bailing.

Behind us, a few people from the overturned raft clung to boulders protruding from the river, and passengers in the other rafts were attempting to rescue them. Two people from the third raft fell into the water while trying to pull someone in.

Wild Man steered us to a rocky clearing. Birch trees surrounded us, creating a barrier from the river. The roar of the water was muffled. The clearing was dark with patches of light piercing through the leaves. The extinguished remains of a campfire were in the center, and a picnic table sat beside it.

Wild Man made a fire and grabbed a sleeping bag from the storage chest. By the time we got things set up, the third raft pulled in, followed quickly by the last one.

Judy walked by with Bernie in tow. I was about to make a snide comment — something witty like "Really fun trip, Judy" — when I noticed she was crying. And Bernie didn't look much better. His face was white, his lips drawn together in a tight, thin line, and he had tears in his eyes too.

"What's wrong? I asked.

Judy turned to me and shrieked, "Kim fell into the river, and we don't know where she is. We have to find her!"

Kim, their teenaged daughter. And my honorary little sister. I tried to say something comforting to Bernie and Judy, but nothing intelligible came out.

Wild Man walked to the center of the group and said, "Alright, listen up. Three people are unaccounted for."

I looked around camp again, this time to see if I could figure out who else was missing. From the corner of my eye, I saw Bernie's arm tighten around Judy's shoulder.

Wild Man continued, "We need to form search par—"

He was interrupted by faint cries from the other side of the river. Two young men and Kim stood shouting to us and waving their arms above their heads to get our attention.

Wild Man ran to the water's edge. He called and motioned to them to meet him upstream at a fork in the river where it was narrow enough to cross. Judy and Bernie jogged along behind, not willing to wait before being reunited with their daughter.

The rest of us turned our attention to warming up the people who'd been in the water. Those of us fortunate enough to have stayed dry removed as much of our clothing as we could for those who needed to change out of wet things. I stripped down to my thermal undershirt, offering up a crewneck sweater, a wool shirt, cotton turtleneck, and thick wool socks.

That left me cold and miserable. I was feeling sorry for myself until I watched one of the women who'd been in the water. She sat shivering and didn't move when a couple of women tried to help her remove her wet things.

"What's your name?" a grandmotherly type asked her.

No reply.

"What is your name?" she asked again, this time with her face inches from the woman.

"Nan-cy," the woman said slowly, her voice quivering with chills.

"Okay, Nancy," she soothed, "we need to get you out of these wet things and into some dry clothes."

"Rest. Want. . . to. . .rest," Nancy replied.

"In a bit. First let's get you dry," she said as she pulled off Nancy's socks. She held up my wool socks, but Nancy weakly pushed them away.

Sue came up behind me and whispered, "She has hypothermia. Her chills, disorientation, fatigue — all classic signs. We have to get her warmed up. Now."

Sue organized a plan for treating Nancy. Once they got her into dry things, they put Nancy in the sleeping bag. Two women got in with her, one on each side, to provide added warmth.

I watched with envy. I was tempted to volunteer for the next shift with Nancy when a woman who'd just finished her stint came up beside me by the fire. "That looks nice and warm," I told her, nodding my head in the direction of the sleeping bag.

"It's not, trust me," she replied as she lit a cigarette. "I thought my husband's cold feet were bad, but this was worse. She's like an ice cube. Look at me, I'm still shivering." She held out the hand holding the cigarette to demonstrate, and it was noticeably shaking.

Well, so much for that idea, I thought. I didn't have enough body heat to keep me from freezing, let alone warm someone else.

One of the guides had hiked to the base camp to send a bus back for us. I wasn't sure how long it had been since he'd left, but I felt certain we should have been picked up by now. "When is that damned bus going to get here?" I asked no one in particular. "Maybe we should go ahead and hike to the road," I continued, thinking the walk would warm me up.

Nobody answered. For a group this size, there was very little conversation. It wasn't until an hour later when the sick and injured had received medical attention and the rest of us were back at the camp having drinks "on the house" — mostly hot cider and coffee — that we started joking about the experience. We could laugh now about people falling overboard. Or complain about being cold or how sore our arms were from all that bailing. Suddenly it all seemed extremely funny.

I overhead a friend of Judy's telling Kim, "Just a pointer, honey — you're supposed to stay in the raft." That brought chuckles from his cohorts and a blush to Kim's cheeks.

Then he moved on to poor Patricia, commenting that "that purple egg" on her forehead would show up nicely in her wedding pictures.

I decided to stay out of the line of fire so I motioned Sue to join me at the end of the bar. We'd just gotten our coffee when Judy walked up. She'd been making the rounds, stopping to chat with everyone. She said happily, "Guess what? The guides have offered to take us out again to make up for the problems today — for free!"

I stared at her, speechless. Was this the same woman who just hours before had been sobbing, fearful for her daughter's safety? I looked down at the rope burn on my hand. I remembered my panic as I was tossed around the raft, my terror as I saw people floating in the frigid water, my sense of helplessness and discomfort at the campsite.

"I don't think so," I said. "Thanks anyway." ⁓

Recommendations for readers interested in Alaska books by and about women

ACCIDENTAL ADVENTURER:
Memoir of the First Woman to Climb Mt. McKinley,
by Barbara Washburn, trade paperback, $16.95

BIRD GIRL & THE MAN WHO FOLLOWED THE SUN:
An Athabascan Indian Legend from Alaska,
by Velma Wallis, hardbound edition, $19.95

COLD RIVER SPIRITS:
The Legacy of an Athabascan-Irish family from Alaska's Yukon River,
by Jan Harper-Haines, hardbound, $19.95

FLY FISHING WOMEN EXPLORE ALASKA,
by Cecilia "Pudge" Kleinkauf, trade paperback, $19.95

GOOD TIME GIRLS OF THE ALASKA-YUKON GOLD RUSH,
by Lael Morgan, trade paperback, $16.95

IDITAROD DREAMS:
A Year in the Life of Sled Dog Racer DeeDee Jonrowe,
by Lew Freedman, trade paperback, $14.95

OUR ALASKA:
Personal Stories about Life in the North,
edited by Mike Doogan, trade paperback, $16.95

RAISING OURSELVES:
A Gwitch'in Coming of Age Story from the Yukon River,
by Velma Wallis, hardbound edition, $19.95

TWO OLD WOMEN:
An Alaska Legend of Betrayal, Courage, and Survival,
by Velma Wallis, hardbound, $16.95

These titles can be found at or special-ordered from your local bookstore. These and other Alaska books can be ordered directly from the publisher by calling 1-800-950-6663, or by visiting www.EpicenterPress.com.